"With the mindset of a coach, the heart of a pastor, and the wisdom of a theologian, Dr. Travis Guse offers a rich exploration of the fruitful interplay of calling and identity for today's Christ-follower. This is a valuable resource for coaching others to find their place in God's world."

—CHAD HALL, PRESIDENT, COACH APPROACH MINISTRIES

"I love the way that Travis Guse utilizes coaching as a tool for personalized discipleship. This is a brilliant strategy! The key contribution of *Who Have You Been Called to Be?* is the way it draws on Martin Luther's theologically rich teaching on vocation to coach people into living out their calling in Christ. If you are committed to discipling others, this book is for you."

—STEVEN D. MATHEWSON, FORMER DIRECTOR, DOCTOR OF MINISTRY PROGRAM, WESTERN SEMINARY, PORTLAND, OREGON

"Perhaps we all set out with a dream of what we want to be and do when we grow up. But how many of us actually become the person we hope to be and do the work we set out to do? And for people of faith, where does God fit in with our vocation? Rev. Dr. Travis Guse offers a practical, wisdom-filled, and Christ-centered path toward vocational discernment. Your most fulfilled self awaits you as you set out on this worthwhile journey with Travis and the timeless wisdom of Protestant Reformer Martin Luther."

—PAUL M. BURNS, PASTOR, COACH, AND AUTHOR *BECOMING SPIRITUALLY INTELLIGENT: NINE PATHS TOWARD YOUR MOST LOVING SELF*

"It only took 500+ years but vocational coaching's time has come! ... Dr. Guse brings decades of pastoral ministry experience together with coaching competency to share a framework that can inspire and rejuvenate Jesus followers on their vocational journey. I recommend this book to anyone who finds themselves and/or members of their faith family searching for greater alignment between their faith and their work."

—JANE CRESWELL, MASTER CERTIFIED COACH, AUTHOR OF *CHRIST-CENTERED COACHING* AND *COACHING FOR EXCELLENCE*

"Blending biblical principles with modern coaching strategies, this book offers practical wisdom grounded in Scripture, and it has reshaped how I approach coaching others. A must read for Christian leaders and mentors!"

—Ben Griffin, CEO of LINC Ministries

"Until recently, so few counselors and coaches have tried to integrate Luther's Christ-centered theology into today's culture and personal concerns. Luther's theology is a soul care theology, and Guse has gifted us with his insights into how that theology can be used to coach people to make wise and faith-filled vocational decisions. I was a career counselor earlier in my life and wish that this book had been available to me then. I am so pleased that Guse has helped to add these badly needed insights."

—Rick Marrs, licensed psychologist, senior professor, Concordia Seminary, St. Louis

"Coaching once saved my vocation as a Christian leader. During a time of disillusionment and even despair, my coach walked with me to a deeper understanding of Christ's gracious call on my life. This thoughtful guide by my classmate and friend, Travis Guse, will help followers of Jesus understand why they need a coach. As a theologian, Travis will also lead you to a transformative understanding of the Bible's teaching on vocation."

—Ben Haupt, global executive director, PLI

Who Have You Been Called to Be?

Who Have You Been Called to Be?

A Study on Coaching and Luther's Teaching on Vocation

TRAVIS GUSE

Foreword by Robert Kolb

WIPF & STOCK · Eugene, Oregon

WHO HAVE YOU BEEN CALLED TO BE?
A Study on Coaching and Luther's Teaching on Vocation

Copyright © 2024 Travis Guse. All rights reserved. Except for brief quotations in critical publications or reviews, no part of this book may be reproduced in any manner without prior written permission from the publisher. Write: Permissions, Wipf and Stock Publishers, 199 W. 8th Ave., Suite 3, Eugene, OR 97401.

Wipf & Stock
An Imprint of Wipf and Stock Publishers
199 W. 8th Ave., Suite 3
Eugene, OR 97401

www.wipfandstock.com

PAPERBACK ISBN: 979-8-3852-2387-9
HARDCOVER ISBN: 979-8-3852-2388-6
EBOOK ISBN: 979-8-3852-2389-3

10/28/24

Gallup, CliftonStrengths and the CliftonStrengths 34 Themes of Talent are trademarks of Gallup, Inc. All rights reserved. The non-Gallup® information you are receiving has not been approved and is not sanctioned or endorsed by Gallup® in any way. Opinions, views and interpretations of CliftonStrengths® are solely the beliefs of the author of this publication.

The non-Gallup information you are receiving has not been approved and is not sanctioned or endorsed by Gallup in any way. Opinions, views, and interpretations of CliftonStrengths are solely the beliefs of Rev. Dr. Travis Guse, the author of this publication.

VIA Institute on Character Copyright 2004–2024, used with permission; all rights reserved. www.viacharacter.org

Myers-Briggs Type Indicator©, Myers-Briggs©, MBTI©, Step I™, Step II™, Step III™, the MBTI logo, and The Myers-Briggs Company logo are trademarks or registered trademarks of Myers & Briggs Foundation in the United States and other countries.

All the coaching stories written in this book are shared with permission by each individual coaching client. These stories are written with the intention of exemplifying the value of coaching in helping someone identify their authentic identity in Christ, empowering them to live out their callings in their various responsibilities, and providing strategies for each person to make a kingdom impact in their respective contexts.

Contents

Foreword by Robert Kolb   vii

Acknowledgments   ix

Preface   xi

1. Introduction: Discovering Our Calling   1
2. Luther's Teaching on Vocation   12
3. Vocational Coaching   57
4. Setting Up the Coaching Project   102
5. Project Results and Interviews   142
6. Application of Vocational Coaching in the Church   159

Appendix   175

Bibliography   177

Foreword

Doctoral dissertations report on extensive research projects that are aimed at providing new information and insights, innovative analyses, approaches, and applications of a particular topic and for specific practices. Pastor Travis Guse has produced just such a study from research conducted on a significant fresh approach to an important element of Christian life together, conversations of encouragement and edification, in this case specifically focused on critical questions of occupational identity.

"What should I do with the rest of my life?" Most people ask themselves—and perhaps even others—that question more than once as the years pass by. According to the philosophy of the psychiatrist Erik Erikson (1902–1994), we all pass through stages of life, with transitions between that pose questions of this sort. This process of questioning, of self-examination, results in a crisis of identity of varying degrees of intensity.

Out of personal experience with the rather recently developed method or technique called "coaching," Pastor Guse studied how methods of personal coaching can be used as instruments of the support system provided within the life of a Christian congregation and its ministry to its community. Having personally benefited from being coached during a period of rethinking his occupational calling and his formal service in Christ's church, Guse probed theoretical and practical examinations of coaching as a tool for effectively providing support for others when they are weighing choices and options while they are going through a period of rethinking their identity and life goals.

Guse recognized a foundation for such coaching in Martin Luther's concept of the Christian's calling from God to live out faith in Christ within the contexts of home, occupation, civil community and organizations, and

FOREWORD

the Christian congregation. In the medieval church in which Luther grew up, the concept of *vocatio* or calling referred only to the commission that God gives to those who formally served the institutional church. Only priests, monks, friars, and nuns could claim a *vocatio*. God was said to have called them to special sacrificial service that led them over a steeper but surer path to God's grace than those involved in other walks of life. Luther transformed the use of the word "calling," or "vocation," into a term that described the source of every aspect of human life: God calls us to serve him by providing for the needs of fellow human beings. Because he judged it "not good" for Adam to be alone, he provided him with a "helper" or "partner" (Gen 2:18, NRSV). Our Creator calls each of us to care for one another in the circles in which he gives us responsibilities—in home and family, in occupation, in political and societal relationships and organizations, and in the company of those with whom we worship him. Luther applied the term not only to the "religious" but to all his people, and he asserted that all have such callings in all four areas of human life.

Against the background of this way of perceiving human life in general and Christian life in particular, Dr. Guse has provided in this project the material that his review of current coaching practices helped him uncover as he conducted his research. He shares it alongside the practical application of his research in his book *Called2B* that leads readers into the practices of Christian coaching. For those who wish to follow his path into the world of Christian coaching and look over his shoulder as he pulls together insights and observations from his research, the dissertation provides details of his method and his findings. Thus, this book extends the impact of Guse's work and offers both pastors and lay people resources for aiding others through times of questioning and crisis grounded on a solid biblical, theological foundation. Guse thus equips readers for serving sisters and brothers in critical times and strengthens their ability to serve the people of God.

ROBERT KOLB

Acknowledgments

I want to take this opportunity to acknowledge the contribution of a few important people in the development and completion of this book. First, I want to thank my wife, Stephanie, without whom I could not have completed this dissertation. She did not give up on me the many times I wanted to give up on myself in this process. Her encouragement and support provided the strength I needed to see this dissertation through to completion. The saying "Behind every great man is a great woman" is so very true when it comes to my wife. I also want to thank my son Kendall for his understanding when I didn't always have the time for him because of the demands of this project. Please know how much I love and appreciate you both.

Additionally, I want to thank my first reader, Dr. Kolb, who has served as a mentor in my love, understanding, and application of our rich Lutheran theological tradition. I want to thank Chad Hall for his leadership as the head of our coaching cohort for my doctoral program at Western Seminary. You have shown me such generosity with your time and I have come to value your deep understanding of the field of coaching.

Besides these individuals, I want to thank the Southeastern District, who provided a sabbatical for me to begin my research for this dissertation, as well as the strong encouragement to complete this program. Special thanks goes to all those in Circuit 10 who participated in my Called2B empowerment events and follow-up coaching—without all of you I could not have completed my dissertation coaching project. And finally, I want to thank my faith family at St. John Lutheran Church in Idaho Falls, Idaho. Thank you for supporting me in my doctoral studies when I served you as your pastor.

Preface

Who am I? Why am I here? What is my purpose? How can I make a more significant impact in the world today? All these questions have to do with the topic of vocation. Vocation is more than what one does for a living in terms of their work or career. Through the lens of Martin Luther's teaching of vocation, believers see the larger story of who they are in terms of their calling with God through faith in Jesus and how they are now called to love and serve their neighbors through all of their areas of responsibility in life. Yet, while this teaching on vocation can be understood biblically and theologically, many believers struggle to discern their calling personally and practically.

This dissertation focuses on how coaching can help empower believers to discern and more intentionally live out their authentic calling in Christ in their daily lives. The developing field of coaching provides a pathway to vocationally disciple Christians to deepen their awareness of their ultimate identity in Christ and better discern their unique identity of God's workmanship and gifting in their life. Coaching can also help believers focus on developing a holistic empowerment plan where they can care for themselves heart, soul, mind, and body to show up at their best in their various callings in life. And finally, coaching can empower believers to make a more significant kingdom impact in their different stations of life—family, church, lifework, and society.

1

Introduction: Discovering Our Calling

SNOOP DOGG AND CALLING

In 2008, one of the members of my congregation in the Thousand Oaks area of California asked me to coach him. He was one of my first coaching clients. He was a young twenty-three-year-old Hollywood producer named Dave.[1] Only the year before he moved to Southern California to work with a production company that had brought him down because of the promise that he had shown. He had grown up Lutheran in the Sacramento area and was active in his faith and the life of the church. Yet, each time Dave went to work, he felt that he was right on the edge when it came to his faith. He didn't find any redemptive value in producing Snoop Dogg videos and the like day in and day out. He often was offered opportunities to shoot porno videos with the assurance that he didn't have to use his real name in the credits.

When Dave shared his conflict with me about his calling in Christ and his work in the entertainment industry, I suggested doing some coaching together. While coaching, like the field of counseling, was developed independently from the sphere of faith, it is a helpful tool for ministry that is being used more and more within the church. A coach works with another person by guiding them through a process that empowers the person being coached to make discoveries, find solutions, and move forward in taking action steps aligned with their vision and goals.[2] Ultimately, the coach

---

1. Story shared with permission.
2. Webb, *COACH Model*, 34.

focuses on a process that allows the coachee to find their own solutions. While counseling is past-oriented and typically aimed at helping those who receive it to find healing, coaching, instead, is future-oriented and aimed at assisting relatively well-adjusted people in developing goals and taking action.³ A key distinction of coaching versus other helping professions like consulting or mentoring is that the expertise lies not with the coach but with the person being coached.⁴ The coach is an expert in the process of coaching, while the client is the expert of their life.

As I started coaching Dave, he wanted to do work in his field that more aligned with his faith and values. So, we took the next three months exploring his various options and developing strategies to make it happen. I also provided him much needed encouragement, support, and gospel accountability along the way. The significant learning for Dave that came out of our coaching together was the idea of living as a servant leader in Hollywood. In Hollywood, the culture is dominated by the attitude "what can you do for me?" Dave began to work with a philosophy of "what can I do for you?" As he sought to love and serve those he met in Hollywood with this approach, people were shocked and surprised, wondering who this guy was. He also prayed for God to open doors for him to be able to live out his faith each day where God had called him in his work. And as he did, Dave won a hearing for the gospel with people that most individuals would never have an opportunity to do. He became an everyday missionary in Hollywood.

Eventually, God opened doors for Dave through this servant leadership approach. In 2013 Dave signed a deal with William Morris Endeavor (WME), the largest talent agency in Hollywood, to start a new faith media company called Freely. This was the first time a talent agency ever launched a new media company, let alone a faith media company. In 2018, Freely launched their first media project, *The Long Goodbye—The Kara Tippits Story*, on Netflix with a slate of new projects lined up for production. While not every coaching relationship produces these kinds of results, this story highlights well the focus on this book. How can we, as the church, empower believers to discover and more intentionally live out their authentic calling in Christ in their everyday areas of responsibility in life for greater kingdom impact?

3. Collins, *Christian Coaching*, 14.
4. Creswell, *Christ-Centered Coaching*, 15.

Introduction: Discovering Our Calling

MY JOURNEY INTO COACHING (MY BACKGROUND)

I discovered the power of coaching for vocational discipleship in 2007. Like Dave, I was also struggling with my own questions of calling after leaving my first pastoral ministry due to some ethical concerns within the church I was serving. Over the next three years, I waited for the Lord's answer as to what the next chapter of my life was going to be. During this time, I experienced depression and hopelessness at a level I had never experienced in my life before. I felt worthless and without a clear sense of direction and purpose in my life. I so wanted to serve again as a pastor, but I received no calls. I still had faith in Jesus, and intellectually believed that he was always there for me, yet his presence felt so distant, and my future was clouded. It was difficult longing for Jesus to reveal the next chapter as I waited upon his perfect timing.

Part of the refining God wanted to do in my life during this time of extended waiting was to help me discover the real basis of my identity. I had not realized how much of my identity had become wrapped up in being a pastor rather than who I was in Christ. When many lose their jobs, especially men, they struggle with their sense of identity and self-worth. The reason for this is because their identity often gets wrapped up in what they do for a living. I was a Christian and had faith in Jesus. Yet, my identity became misplaced over time. It gradually became more about what I did rather than whose I was. God used this wilderness experience as a crucible moment so that I would discover, once more, that my true calling was in Jesus alone as a child of God. Though this was one of the most painful experiences in my life, I am a much better pastor as a result of it because of God's working in my life during this time.

It was during this wilderness experience that I also discovered coaching. It happened when I took the Gallup® StrengthsFinder (now known as CliftonStrengths®)[5] assessment at a church in Los Angeles, called Mosaic, as part of a leadership development event they were hosting. This assessment tool is designed to help people identify their natural talents and develop them to build a strengths-based life.[6] Through the experience, I suddenly gained a better understanding and articulation of God's unique workmanship in my life. Taking the assessment highlighted for me that there are things that are

---

5. Gallup®, CliftonStrengths® and the CliftonStrengths 34 Themes of Talent are trademarks of Gallup, Inc. All rights reserved.

6. Gallup, "Learn How."

true about ourselves that, sometimes, we can't see. Others may be able to see it, but we are blind to this truth. Or there are things we know about ourselves that others don't. That was the case when it came to some of my greatest God-given talents and strengths. These God-given talents were there, yet I didn't have the awareness to understand how they contributed to making me uniquely me, or the articulation to describe them to others. Through this assessment I found value in myself again and regained a sense that, in Christ, God had created and gifted me for a purpose in this life.

During that time of wandering, I had a fantastic coach, whose name was Mike Ruhl. Mike walked with me through that wilderness experience, listened to me, and asked great coaching questions that provided me with a perspective beyond the depression I was experiencing. Through our work together, I gained a greater awareness that my true calling and identity was in Christ, not in what I did for a living. We celebrated together these newfound strengths in my life and envisioned how God might desire to work through them so that I could be a greater blessing to others. He also worked with me to develop a strategy that empowered me to step into that new vision that Christ was calling me towards, especially concerning my life as a pastor and now as a coach. While Mike provided pastoral care to me during this time, his coaching also empowered me to better discern and live out my authentic calling in Christ in my daily life as I waited on God to unfold the next chapter of life and ministry. God powerfully used Mike through his encouragement and support to remind me that I was not alone.

Soon after these experiences, I was trained to be a certified Gallup® Strengths Coach.[7] I continued through a series of coach training programs, next with the College of Executive Coaching, in which I trained to be an executive life coach. Then I was certified as a mission coach through CoachNet and our Center for US Missions in the Lutheran Church–Missouri Synod (LCMS). Besides being a pastor, I am currently a professional certified coach (PCC) accredited with the International Coach Federation (ICF) and serve as a coach trainer with Coach Approach Ministries. Now, through coaching, I seek to empower everyday believers to discover and live out their authentic calling in Christ. In my current role as the Executive Director of Wellness and Coaching for the Southeastern District (LCMS), I utilize coaching with individuals and groups seeking to discern God's calling for their lives and ministries and developing action plans to live those out.

---

7. Gallup®, CliftonStrengths® and the CliftonStrengths 34 Themes of Talent are trademarks of Gallup, Inc. All rights reserved.

INTRODUCTION: DISCOVERING OUR CALLING

Over the last two decades since becoming a coach, I have found coaching to be a powerful approach for personally discipling believers to better comprehend their Christian vocation in life. While preaching and teaching Bible studies are powerful tools for discipling others in their faith walk with Jesus, as a pastor, I would often feel like these were a shotgun approach where I just hoped that I would hit someone's mind and heart. However, coaching provides a personalized process to disciple people in a laser-focused way that assists them in translating all those sermons, Bible studies, and time in God's word into personal application and action, especially when it comes to living out their vocation in Christ. Coaching serves to empower believers, not simply to be hearers of the word but doers of the word as well (Jas 1:22).

BOOK FOCUS

The focus of this book is on how coaching can serve as a means to empower believers to better discern and more intentionally live out their authentic calling in Christ in their daily lives. This research focus is vital to me for two reasons. The first is personal, coming from the standpoint of my struggles in the past with discerning my calling in life so long ago. The second comes from the work I have done in coaching with hundreds of individuals as they have searched for clarity regarding their calling in life as well. Often, these coaching conversations ultimately revolve around the following questions of their souls: "Who am I?"; "Why am I here?"; "What is life all about?"; "What am I supposed to do?"; and "How can I make a greater impact?" In my experience these are, ultimately, questions of vocation, which, I have found, coaching so effectively helps people address.

This book is seeking to address three significant problems within the church in helping believers of all ages discover and live out their vocation in life. The first is that many believers do not have an over-arching biblical and theological framework for understanding who they are and their place in the world. According to Barna, only 10 percent of boomers, 7 percent of Gen X, 6 percent of millennials, and 4 percent of Gen Z have a biblical worldview.[8]

---

8. Barna Group and Impact 360, *Gen Z*, 113; Barna defines one who holds a "biblical worldview" by the following factors: (1) has made a personal commitment to Jesus that is still important in their life today; (2) believes they will go to heaven when they die "because you have confessed your sins and accepted Jesus Christ as your Savior"; (3) strongly agrees the Bible is totally accurate in all of its teachings; (4) strongly agrees they personally have a responsibility to tell other people your religious beliefs; (5) strongly

Who Have You Been Called to Be?

As we become more and more a post-church and post-Christian society, even those within our churches often do not have the biblical literacy to address the deep questions of meaning and purpose that they are wrestling with today.

The second problem is that one of our rich theological frameworks that we have to address these questions of everyday faith and life has been stripped of its richness and depth in modern times. That framework is Luther's teaching on vocation. Unfortunately, today, vocation is just merely another term referring to one's job or career training. However, during the Reformation, Luther's understanding of vocation was one that encompassed a comprehensive view of life. It provides answers to questions about our ultimate identity, our place in the world, and how we are to navigate our various areas of responsibilities in life. Without this robust theological framework, many are left to look to other competing worldviews or solely to themselves as the defining narrative to guide them in life.

The third problem I'm seeking to address is that there is, often, little attention given to personally disciple believers on how to connect the dots between their faith and the rest of life. Sunday after Sunday, the faithful hear that they are loved and forgiven by Jesus, with little attention given to what that means for their personal life. And when pastors do address practical steps for living one's faith in the world, these words are, often, too over-generalized to apply to the hearer's context. For example, when it comes to work, a recent Barna study reveals that while nearly two-thirds of Christians believe that God gave them specific talents and gifts to use for his glory, one-third want a clearer vision on how they should use these gifts and talents.[9] And less than half of millennials feel their church gives them a vision for living out their faith at work. For Gen Z, 57 percent feel this same way.[10]

---

disagrees that Jesus Christ committed sins when he lived on earth; (6) strongly disagrees that the devil, or Satan, is not a living being but a symbol of evil; (7) strongly disagrees that a person can earn a place in heaven if they are generally good or they do enough good things for others; and (8) believes God is the all-powerful, all-knowing, perfect creator of the universe who rules the world today.

9. Barna Group, *Christians at Work*, 25.
10. Barna Group, *Christians at Work*, 81.

Introduction: Discovering Our Calling

WHY IS THIS STUDY NEEDED?

The reason for this study is that there is no other treatment, that I am aware of, that directly makes the connection between Luther's theologically rich teaching on vocation and how coaching can help individuals step into this vision for their lives in a personalized way. While much has been written on the subject of vocation from historical and theological perspectives, what has been missing is a personal and practical application. How do we not only help believers to see God's framework for understanding who they are and what life is all about but also then empower them to live this calling out in the contexts where God has called them to in life? It is this connection that I believe will bear much fruit in the lives of those within our churches who are seeking to make a more significant kingdom impact in their areas of responsibility.

David Kinnaman addresses this desperate need for a new approach to vocational discipleship, especially with younger generations, in his book *You Lost Me*. The problem, he asserts, is that we have tended towards discipleship in a mass-production, one-size-fits-all approach. But in his view, ". . . disciples cannot be mass-produced. Disciples are handmade, one relationship at a time."[11] According to Kinnaman, "We need new ecosystems of spiritual and vocational apprenticeship that can support deeper relationships and more vibrant faith formation. . . . We need to renew our catechisms and confirmations—not because we need new theology, but because their current forms too rarely produce young people of deep, abiding faith."[12] The sad reality is the church is not discipling these young believers in a way that prepares them to live out their faith in Jesus in the world they are experiencing today. From my training and experience, coaching provides just such an approach.

PURPOSE OF THIS STUDY

The purpose of this study is to demonstrate how coaching can help people personally discover and more intentionally live out their authentic calling in Christ in their various areas of responsibility in life. I will first examine how Luther's teaching on vocation can provide a framework for the life of a believer to answer some of the deep questions of life and faith. Second, I will

---

11. Kinnaman, *You Lost Me*, 13.
12. Kinnaman, *You Lost Me*, 13.

explore how coaching can serve as a personalized discipleship approach to empower believers to apply and live out this valuable theological framework for their life. Third, I will synthesize my research on Luther's teaching on vocation and coaching to create a biblically and theologically grounded coaching framework to empower believers to more intentionally discover and live out their authentic calling in Christ. Fourth, I will conduct a research study with congregational members of a grouping of churches in the greater Richmond, Virginia, area to validate the effectiveness of coaching for vocational discipleship. Lastly, I will examine the results of this study and make recommendations for how coaching can be utilized by ministries to personally disciple those who want to more intentionally integrate their faith and life.

RESEARCH QUESTIONS

The following are some of the research questions I intend to try to answer in the course of this book:

1. What does "vocation" mean, and how should we understand it from a biblical and theological standpoint?
2. How does the theological framework of vocation answer the big questions people are asking in life?
3. What is coaching, and what is not coaching?
4. Can coaching effectively be used as a practical approach to personally empower believers to discover and live out their authentic calling in Christ in their various domains in life?
5. How can coaching connect one's ultimate calling in Christ with one's daily life in a comprehensive way?
6. Why is coaching an especially effective approach for discipling younger generations as opposed to more commonly used delivery approaches for discipleship that we see in the church today?
7. Why is coaching needed today, and why is it essential for both believers and for the church?
8. What can coaching do and what can't it do?
9. What does coaching for vocational discipleship look like practically?
10. What will be lost if I don't answer these questions?

Introduction: Discovering Our Calling

KEY TERMS

Vocation—Latin for "calling." While often used today to refer to one's career, biblically and theologically, it encompasses all of one's stations in life (active righteousness) as well as one's calling by grace through faith in Christ (passive righteousness). A more comprehensive understanding of Luther's teaching on vocation will be explored in chapter 2, "Luther's Teaching on Vocation—The World According to God."

Coaching—The International Coach Federation (ICF) defines coaching as "partnering with clients in a thought-provoking and creative process that inspires them to maximize their personal and professional potential, which is particularly important in today's uncertain and complex environment."[13] A more comprehensive understanding of coaching, especially within the context of Luther's understanding of vocation, will be explored in chapter 3, "Vocational Coaching—Finding My Place in the World."

PBC—Person Being Coached, also known as a "coachee" or "client."

ASSUMPTIONS OF THIS STUDY

I want to acknowledge up front that I have a particular presupposition that I bring to my book. While I will approach this discussion from a Christocentric and gospel-centered perspective that many in the Christian tradition embrace, I have to be honest that I do so through a specific theological lens. As a pastor in the Lutheran tradition, I have a well-defined theological tradition that informs how I see Jesus and the Scriptures. With this, I assume that humanity is not basically good, but, rather, separated from God and others. As Luther taught, we are "turned in" on ourselves, loving ourselves at the exclusion of our Creator and our neighbor. As such, we are in need of a Savior to redeem and restore us rightly in these two fundamental relationships that were intended for us since the creation. This will significantly impact how I approach coaching, which tends to see people as basically whole.

I will also approach this project through the lens of the great Solas of the Lutheran Reformation—*Sola Gratia* (grace alone), *Sola Fide* (faith alone), *Sola Scriptura* (Scripture alone)—and, ultimately, *Sola Christus* (Christ alone). Through this solidly Lutheran lens, I will uplift the importance of

---

13. ICF, "What Is Professional Coaching?"

each believer's baptismal identity as their ultimate identity in Christ. I will also utilize the theological frameworks of Luther's teaching on Law and Gospel, as well as his teaching on the Two Kinds of Righteousness. Lastly, I will specifically be approaching my discussion of vocation through the rich theological teaching of Dr. Martin Luther's perspective on the topic.

BOUNDARIES OF THIS STUDY

With the previous assumptions laid out, there are going to be some boundaries that are going to be essential to maintain in my book's focus. I will not be able to provide a comprehensive overview of the doctrine of vocation across various Christian traditions over the twenty centuries of the church. For the sake of this book, I will be focusing on Martin Luther's understanding and teaching on vocation.[14] Part of the reason for this delineation is because there is, frankly, too much material to try to cover if I took a broad overview across theological backgrounds. The other is because of my theological affinity, being a Lutheran pastor.

Another reason for this delineation is a personal one. I firmly believe that we in the tradition of Luther have something vital to contribute to the meaningful conversation that is taking place about vocation today in the Church. Often those in my theological tradition have had a "circle-the-wagon" mentality where we tend to keep to ourselves in order to keep our theology "pure." Yet, it is my personal conviction that we who subscribe to the Lutheran tradition have much to offer the wider Church, especially in regard to our well-developed teaching on vocation. This doctrine can be a blessing to the greater body of Christ at this critical time in the history of the Church.

The last boundary that I will seek to keep is regarding how I approach my discussion on the field of coaching in this study. While an exploration of how coaching can serve as an applied side approach in helping believers in vocational discernment and empowerment, this is not going to be a comprehensive "how-to" book on coaching. As mentioned before, there are many fantastic books, resources, and training programs out there on how

---

14. Calvin also made a rich theological contribution to the Protestant concept of vocation. An example of this is when he teaches that "the Lord bides each one of us in all life's actions to look to his calling.... Therefore each individual has his own kind of living assigned to him by the Lord as a sort of sentry post so that he may not heedlessly wander about throughout life." Calvin, "Institutes," 236–37.

INTRODUCTION: DISCOVERING OUR CALLING

to be an effective coach, especially from a Christian perspective. But, for the sake of this book, I am going to focus specifically on how coaching can help believers discover their authentic calling in Christ and empower them to this calling in their various areas of responsibility in life.

IMPORTANCE OF THIS STUDY

It is my hope and prayer that this study will be a blessing not only to the Church at large but specifically to individual believers who are lacking a larger biblical and theological framework to answer the big questions of life: "Who am I?"; "Why am I here?"; "What is life about?"; "What am I to do?"; and "How do I make a difference?" With a growing lack of biblical literacy because of the secularization of our society, many of God's people are left with few tools to address questions regarding their identity, security, and meaning in life. Through this study, I am hoping to help new generations reclaim this theological framework of vocation that, for Luther, was intended to define and guide the life of a believer in all of their areas of responsibility in life.

Yet, knowledge does not equate to understanding, let alone implementation. The thoroughly Lutheran question "What does this mean?" not only evokes a search for deeper spiritual contemplation regarding Luther's teaching on vocation but also stirs within the heart of the questioner a desire for personal application. The typical delivery approaches of discipleship, that of preaching and teaching, has not led to the transformation nor empowerment of individual believers in how they live a purpose-filled life. It is my conviction and experience that a discovery approach like coaching can serve as an effective way to personally disciple individuals when it comes to their calling in life. For those who want to begin the journey to discover and live out who they have been created and now redeemed to be in Christ, coaching can be a powerful approach to help them do this with greater intentionality in their lives.

2

Luther's Teaching on Vocation

THE WORLD ACCORDING TO GOD

In her book *The Great Emergence* Phyllis Tickle makes the case that every five hundred years or so the church holds a rummage sale.[1] The purpose, she argues, is so that a revitalized expression of the Christian faith emerges, and the gospel is released to transform lives and cultures. Still, in a rummage sale, not everything is sold or discarded. Sometimes treasures long-forgotten are rediscovered. Like *Antiques Roadshow*, there can be valuable discoveries of items that turn out to have incredible worth. Could such an item exist in the attic of the church today?

With the five-hundredth anniversary of the Lutheran Reformation having taken place in 2017, perhaps now is the time to go through our theological attic to see if just such an item of value needs to be rediscovered for our day. With the nailing of his Ninety-five Theses, Martin Luther sparked a reformation that reclaimed three long-forgotten teachings from Scripture that endure to this day as the bedrock of many denominational traditions: (1) Justification by Grace through Faith; (2) the authority of the Word of God; and (3) the Priesthood of All Believers. However, I believe there was a fourth teaching that has not been fully appreciated for its true value and worth. And this teaching may be just what we need to navigate this post-church and post-Christian culture we find ourselves in today. That teaching is Luther's teaching on vocation.

---

1. Tickle, *Great Emergence*, 16–17.

Luther's Teaching on Vocation

Why is this teaching of Luther's so needed again in our day and age? It is because of the situation many believers find themselves in, in today's culture, as they try to navigate life as a follower of Jesus. Gene Edward Veith makes a case for this need in his book *God at Work* when he states, "Modernity drained any trace of God—even any trace of meaning from the objective world."[2] Veith continues this thought by arguing that faith may be OK for private belief, but it is generally accepted in our culture today, in the North American context, that it has no place in the rest of life. As a result, many are left to navigate this meaningless existence, needing to create meaning in life on their own.[3] Without an overarching framework to provide definition, life can appear meaningless, leaving individuals hopeless and lost as they try to navigate it.

According to Robert Bellah and his co-authors in the book *Habits of the Heart*, the framework that our culture offers as an alternative to faith for navigating life is a combination of "utilitarian individualism" and "expressive individualism."[4] Robert Benne, in his book *Ordinary Saints*, explores the promises made by these two alternative frameworks for life suggested by Bellah. Utilitarian individualism, he states, promises success in life, yet often at the expense of personal relationships.[5] Expressive individualism promotes self-expression and self-definition, yet often at the expense of cultural norms and traditions.[6] Both forms of individualism leave people to be the final author and authority of their own lives. What works and what feels good are the ultimate guiding principles to navigating life and finding meaning.

However, it is Luther's teaching on vocation that offers a far more fulfilling and significant framework for the life of a believer than just living for themselves, their desires, and their dreams. In his article "Vocation vs. Narcissus" journalist and Lutheran lay theologian Uwe Siemon-Netto makes this case when he argues,

> The specifically Lutheran doctrine of vocation is the most effective antidote against this destructive Zeitgeist because it directs the individual to the "You," the other person, and therefore away from the "Me." The doctrine of vocation stresses the Priesthood

---

2. Veith, *God at Work*, 26.
3. Veith, *God at Work*, 26.
4. Bellah et al., *Habits of the Heart*, 33.
5. Benne, *Ordinary Saints*, 8.
6. Benne, *Ordinary Saints*, 9–10.

of All Believers in the temporal world, where all have a call from God to serve their neighbor in all their everyday endeavors. By doing this in a spirit of love Christians render the highest possible service to God.[7]

It is through Luther's concept of vocation that we can once again move away from the me-ism that so defines our culture today and reclaim a road map for understanding ourselves and our place in the world in relation to God and others. This comprehensive framework to faith and life is what believers must develop within themselves if they are going to engage their world today in a faithful way.[8] As Benne maintains, "Serious Christians fit themselves into the ongoing Christian narrative, one that they believe will not end with this life. Further, they believe that they fit themselves into roles in a drama that God is writing. They freely claim the destiny God offers them. They have robust identities based on the ongoing tradition that defines them."[9] As such, we are transferred from "the world according to me" and into "the world according to God" through this understanding of vocation that Luther developed five centuries ago.

LUTHER'S TEACHING ON VOCATION

Luther's teaching on vocation has a much broader vision than today's contemporary notion of vocation. As Veith explains, Luther's teaching on vocation is more than just about work; it comprises "a theology of Christian life."[10] It is a comprehensive view of daily living that encompasses all of life, from one's relationships with others to one's daily responsibilities.[11] Veith expounds on this when he writes, "But more than that, the doctrine of vocation amounts to a comprehensive doctrine of Christian life, having to do with faith and sanctification, grace and good works. It is the key to Christian ethics. It shows how Christians can influence their culture. It transfigures ordinary, everyday life with the presence of God."[12] In short, Luther's understanding of vocation serves as a framework for believers to understand one's meaning and purpose in all of life.

7. Siemon-Netto, "Vocation vs. Narcissus," 1.
8. Benne, *Ordinary Saints*, 52.
9. Benne, *Ordinary Saints*, 7.
10. Veith, *God at Work*, 133.
11. Veith, *God at Work*, 133.
12. Veith, *God at Work*, 17.

Luther's Teaching on Vocation

Widely recognized as the most authoritative work on Luther's theological teaching on vocation is Gustaf Wingren's *Luther on Vocation*.[13] In it, Wingren explains that the essential biblical lens through which Luther viewed vocation was 1 Cor 7:20.[14] In this passage, the apostle Paul asserts, "Each one should remain in the condition in which he was called" (1 Cor 7:20–21 ESV). In this passage Paul encourages believers to primarily focus on the responsibilities God has given them each day. Here Luther biblically establishes his meaning in regards to his concept of vocation as he explains that everyone has a station or "stand" in life; an area of responsibility derived from one's relationships in life.[15] As such, vocation, at its core, is a relational structure that gives meaning and purpose to life, expressing God's will for the human family.

In his article entitled "Luther on Vocation," Karlfried Froehlich explains that the word "vocation" is derived from the Latin word *vocatio*, which means "to call" or "calling."[16] Before Luther, "to call" (*vocatio*) was the Latin equivalent from Paul's use of the Greek word *klesis*, which he uses eleven times in his Epistles. It is *klesis* that is primarily understood as the word used for becoming a Christian.[17] However, in 1 Cor 7:20, Paul uses a different Greek word for "to call," the word *kaleo*, which refers, in this context, to one's calling to carry out their tasks or responsibilities in life.[18] It is both of these Greek words that Luther uses to frame his understanding and teaching on vocation.

From his study, Wingren notes that Luther develops two primary uses of the word "vocation": (1) the sharing of the gospel, through which believers are called to be "children of God," and (2) the work one does in their daily areas of responsibility in life.[19] Vocation also has a third use of calling an individual into the Office of the Public Ministry. Luther translates the word "vocation" into the German word *Beruf*.[20] While not rejecting, at all, the spiritual dimension of God calling believers through the gospel, it was this new notion of *Beruf*, as areas of responsibilities or "stations" in life, that

---

13. Kolden, "Luther on Vocation," 383.
14. Wingren, *Luther on Vocation*, 1–2.
15. Wingren, *Luther on Vocation*, 3.
16. Froehlich, "Luther on Vocation," 196.
17. Froehlich, "Luther on Vocation," 197.
18. Louw and Nida, *Greek-English Lexicon*, 423.
19. Wingren, *Luther on Vocation*, 1.
20. Wingren, *Luther on Vocation*, 2.

Who Have You Been Called to Be?

Luther used to counter the general notion of vocation within the Church and society in his day.[21] Luther refers to vocation in this new way of understanding when he emphatically states,

> But in a matter apart from conscience, when outward duties must be performed, then, whether you are a preacher, a magistrate, a husband, a teacher, a pupil, etc., this is no time to listen to the Gospel. You must listen to the Law and follow your vocation.[22]

This reimagined use of the word "vocation" would not only transform how everyday believers saw their stations in life but it would also reshape the social and spiritual structures of the day.

What follows in this chapter is a comprehensive overview of Luther's teaching on the biblical and theological understanding of vocation. As I lay out Luther's understanding of vocation and how it applies to the lives of everyday believers, I will explain how it can serve as an overall framework for better understanding one's calling and purpose in life. As a guide in this endeavor, Marc Kolden's summary of Gustaf Wingren's interpretation of Luther's theological framework on vocation is helpful in understanding this deeply complex teaching better:

> Vocation belongs to our situation between baptism and the final resurrection—a situation in which there are two kingdoms (earth and heaven, in Luther's terminology), two contending powers (God and the devil), two antagonistic components within the Christian person (the old self and the new self), and when Christians are involved in constant struggle. Vocation is our calling in our situation in life, through which we serve God's creative work by being under the law. It is the place in which the person of faith chooses sides in the ongoing combat between God and Satan. The "old self" must bear vocation's cross as long as life on earth lasts and the battle against the devil continues. After death there will be a new kingdom free from the cross, heaven will take the place of earth, and the "new self" will be raised from the dead.[23]

This summary of Kolden's will be flushed out in what follows, but here is a diagram that I created that I hope serves to communicate Luther's understanding and teaching of vocation visually in a clear and concise way:

21. Froehlich, "Luther on Vocation," 200.
22. Luther, "Lectures on Galatians," 117.
23. Kolden, "Luther on Vocation," 383.

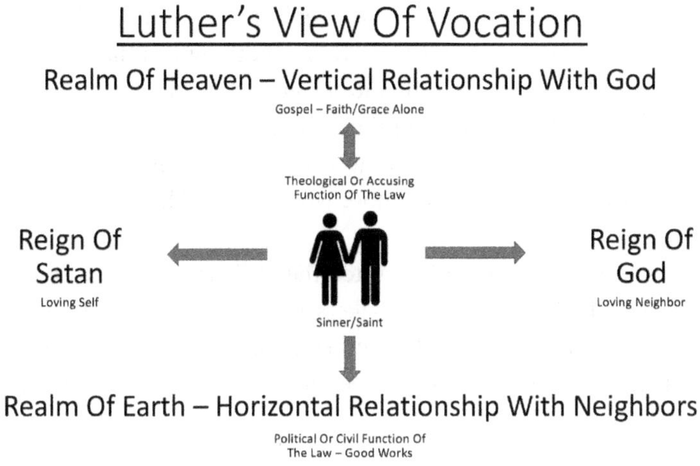

Luther's View Of Vocation

Realm Of Heaven – Vertical Relationship With God
Gospel – Faith/Grace Alone

↑

Theological Or Accusing
Function Of The Law

Reign Of Satan ← 👫 → Reign Of God
Loving Self   Sinner/Saint   Loving Neighbor

↓

Realm Of Earth – Horizontal Relationship With Neighbors
Political Or Civil Function Of
The Law – Good Works

Figure 1. Luther's View of Vocation

From Monastery to Life

Before Luther, the commonly understood notion of having a vocation meant that one was called to be a priest, a monk, or a nun. These individuals, called by the church, often lived isolated from society as they served God with their prayers and devotion. The consensus was that everyday believers did not have a divine call—only those called to "holy" ministry. As Veith notes, "To serve God fully, to live a life that is truly spiritual required full-time commitment."[24] Even marriage and parenthood were seen as getting in the way of living a spiritual life, so living a celibate life was elevated.[25] Unfortunately, as Marc Kolden notes in his book *The Christian's Calling in the World*, this caused many to put faith in good works and monastic vows rather than trusting in God's grace through faith for their salvation.[26]

As Kolden notes, with Luther's rediscovery of the gospel of grace alone, by faith alone, as the only way one is made right with God, this caused him to rethink his view on vocation in general and his calling as a monk specifically.[27] With salvation secured by Christ through faith alone, believers

---

24. Veith, *God at Work*, 18.
25. Vieth, *God at Work*, 18.
26. Kolden, *Christian's Calling*, 6.
27. Kolden, *Christian's Calling*, 7.

were free to direct their good works, instead, toward one's neighbors, which made monastic life unnecessary.[28] As Veith, in his book *Working for Our Neighbor*, explains, "For Luther vocation is nothing less than the locus of the Christian life. God works in and through vocation, but he does so by calling human beings to work in their vocations."[29] This understanding of vocation transformed how Luther saw the everyday lives of believers—they had a vocation as well, not just those who serve in "holy" callings within the Church.

This teaching of Luther's elevated the ordinary tasks and routines in the daily life of peasants, farmers, bakers, woodworkers, parents, husbands, and wives into something godly. Luther expounds on this notion on this spiritual calling of every believer when he writes to the Christian nobility in the German nations:

> It is pure invention that pope, bishops, priests and monks are to be called the "spiritual estate"; princes, lords, artisans, and farmers the "temporal estate." That is indeed a fine bit of lying and hypocrisy. Yet no one should be frightened by it; and for this reason—namely, that all Christians are truly of the "spiritual estate," and there is among them no difference at all but that of office, as Paul says in 1 Cor 12:12: We are all one body, yet every member has its own work, whereby it serves every other, all because we have one baptism, one gospel, one faith, and are all alike Christians; for baptism, gospel and faith alone make us "spiritual" and Christian people.[30]

Before God, all believers are the same through the call of the gospel. As a result, there is no difference between "spirituals" and "temporals" as all their work are holy in the eyes of God.[31] From Luther's perspective, the only difference is the type of work that each one is called to in their various stations in life.

Baptism and Priesthood

The foundation for Luther's understanding of vocation was firmly grounded in his understanding of baptism and the Priesthood of All Believers. He

---

28. Kolden, *Christian's Calling*, 8.
29. Veith, *Working for Our Neighbor*, 14.
30. Luther, "Open Letter," 211.
31. Luther, "Open Letter," 213.

states again in his letter to the German nobility, "Through baptism all of us are consecrated to the priesthood, as St. Peter says in 1 Pet 2:9, 'Ye are a royal priesthood, a priestly kingdom,' and the book of Revelation says, 'Thou hast made us by thy blood to be priests and kings' (5:10)."[32] For Luther, a holy identity was bestowed upon believers through baptism; that of being the royal priesthood. According to Veith, the Priesthood of All Believers is related to, and largely synonymous with, Luther's theological understanding of vocation.[33] It is from this baptismal identity of being part of the royal priesthood that every believer's work and station in life was now considered a sacred calling before God.[34]

However, for Luther, simply having this baptism identity that made all of life something holy did not mean that everyone now held the Office of the Public Ministry. Luther explains this when he writes, "For whoever comes out of the water of baptism can boast that he is already consecrated priest, bishop and pope, though it is not seemly that everyone should exercise the office. . . . For what is common to all, no one dare take upon himself without the will and the command of the community."[35] While one may feel an internal calling to serve as a pastor, such a responsibility must be confirmed by the invitation of the Church into that station in life. For Luther, this was true of the Office of Public Ministry—that believers needed the confirmation of a local community of faith to serve as a pastor, even though they were a part of the Priesthood of All Believers.

Nevertheless, what Luther's teaching on vocation, as related to the Priesthood of All Believers, did was to take the principle of *ora et labora* ("work" and "pray"), found in the monastery, and apply it to the everyday life of believers.[36] This principle did not do away with the Office of the Public Ministry, for pastors and church workers were still necessary for the care of souls within the Church of Christ. But instead, it confirmed that all believers had a sacred calling no matter their stations in life.[37] And as a result, no longer was the monastery the only place that one could serve God with their life. They could do so also as bakers, blacksmiths, farmers, midwifes, and the like.

32. Luther, "Open Letter," 212.
33. Veith, *Working for Our Neighbor*, 33.
34. Veith, *God at Work*, 19.
35. Luther, "Open Letter," 212.
36. Veith, *Working for Our Neighbor*, 38.
37. Veith, *God at Work*, 18–19.

All Vocations Are Holy

As a result of Luther's teachings on vocation, baptism, and the royal priesthood, he affirms that all callings, or stations in life, are holy for believers. Even so, we find many in our churches today who still believe, five hundred years later, that pastors and church workers have "holy callings," while those who are accountants or school janitors do not.[38] Luther firmly counters this notion so prevalent among believers today when he explains,

> How is it possible that you are not called? You have always been in some state or station; you have always been a husband or wife, or boy or girl, or servant. Picture before you the humblest estate. Are you a husband, and you think you have not enough to do in that sphere to govern your wife, children, domestics, and property so that all may be obedient to God and you do no one any harm? Yea, if you had five heads and ten hands, even then you would be too weak for your task, so that you would never dare to think of making a pilgrimage or doing any kind of saintly work.[39]

For Luther, the point is this—whoever you are as a believer and wherever you are; there you have a calling.[40] A believer's calling is literally as far as their eyes can see and as far as their hands can reach. That is one's vocation given by God today.

Not only do believers often have, at times, multiple callings in life, but even the lowliest and most mundane of responsibilities in life are holy. Luther highlights in his "Large Catechism" that even the household chores of a servant girl, when done in faith, is better than the holiness of a monk:

> If these could be impressed on the poor people, a servant girl would dance for joy and praise and thank God; and with her careful work, for which she receives sustenance and wages, she would obtain a treasure such as those who are regarded as the greatest saints do not have. It is not a tremendous honor to know this and to say, "If you do your daily household chores, that is better than the holiness and austere life of all the monks?" Moreover, you have the promise that whatever you do will prosper and fare well. How could you be more blessed or lead a holier life, as far as works are concerned?[41]

---

38. Barna Group, *Christians at Work*, 31.
39. Luther quoted in Kolden, "Luther on Vocation," 383.
40. Kolden, *Christian's Calling*, 27.
41. Luther, "Large Catechism," 406.

For Luther, it is not the type of work that one does that makes a calling or a work holy. It is faith alone that does. Faith alone is the agent that sanctifies the ordinary and transforms it into something sacred in the sight of God. Good works, then, are directed not toward God to make one righteous but in love and service to neighbor, because one is already made righteous by faith.

As such, faith can take even the lowliest station in life and fill it with divine meaning and purpose, while at the same time, releasing the believer to focus instead on loving and serving others rather than trying to love and serve God. Therefore, Luther would advise a believer searching to do something significant for God to stay where they are, for they have a holy calling in their current areas of responsibility in life:

> Therefore I advise no one to enter any religious order or the priesthood, indeed, I advise everyone against it—unless he is forearmed with this knowledge and understands that the works of monks and priests, however holy and arduous they may be, do not differ one whit in the sight of God from the works of the rustic laborer in the field or the woman going about her household tasks, but that all works are measured before God by faith alone.[42]

In our day there is still a temptation to think of what happens in the Church as "sacred," and to see the rest of life as "secular." What Luther is saying here is that all of life is sacred from God's perspective and all of the areas of responsibility in the life of believers are holy as a result.

Serving and Loving Our Neighbors

At the heart of Luther's teaching on vocation is the simple truth that all of a believer's callings in life are for the singular purpose of loving and serving their neighbor. Wingren summarizes this central theme of Luther's theological understanding of vocation when he explains, "It is the neighbor who stands at the center of Luther's ethics, not God's kingdom or God's law or 'character.' Vocation and law benefit the neighbor, as does love born of faith. The same God works through both, in law and vocation without his Spirit, in love born of faith with his Spirit."[43] What Wingren is expressing is the notion that whether or not the motivation comes from the law working through the demands of one's responsibilities in life, or love, motivated by

---

42. Luther, "Word and Sacrament II," 78.
43. Wingren, *Luther on Vocation*, 46.

faith, it is the service of neighbor that is the focus of the believer's callings in life. Wingren affirms this truth of Luther's teaching when he writes, "When the work of vocation is carried out, the neighbor is profited."[44]

In his work "The Freedom of the Christian" Luther lays out this overarching vision for believers of serving one's neighbor through their vocation when he writes,

> Man, however, needs none of these things for his righteousness and salvation. Therefore, he should be guided in all his works by this thought and contemplate this one thing alone, that he may serve and benefit others in all that he does, considering nothing except the need and the advantage of his neighbor.[45]

This idea counters both the monastic ideal of Luther's day that one could win God's approval through a life of devotion to him and our current culture's self-focused vision of living for oneself. Luther's teaching on vocation echoes Paul's exhortation regarding God's will for the life of believers when he writes, "For the whole law is fulfilled in one word: 'You shall love your neighbor as yourself'" (Gal 5:20 ESV). As believers hear this scriptural call to love one's neighbor, it prompts within them that question of the expert of the law asking Jesus, "And who is my neighbor?" (Luke 10:29 NIV) Ultimately, every vocation has a particular neighbor whom one is called, by God, to serve.[46]

As many believers were engaging with God's word thanks to the Reformation, some began to question if there were some careers that one should not participate in due to this scriptural call to love one's neighbor.[47] Can a Christian serve as a judge? A hangman? A soldier? Luther addresses this question in a short work entitled "Whether Soldiers, Too, Can Be Saved," when he explains,

> Now slaying and robbing do not seem to be works of love. A simple man therefore does not think it is a Christian thing to do. In truth, however, even this is a work of love. For example, a good doctor sometimes finds so serious and terrible a sickness that he must amputate or destroy a hand, foot, ear, eye, to save the body. Looking at it from the point of view of the organ that he amputates, he appears to be a cruel and merciless man; but looking at it

---

44. Wingren, *Luther on Vocation*, 125.
45. Luther, "Freedom of a Christian," 617.
46. Veith, *Working for Our Neighbor*, 14–15.
47. Veith, *God at Work*, 9.

> from the point of view of the body, which the doctor wants to save, he is a fine and true man and does a good and Christian work, as far as the work itself is concerned. In the same way, when I think of a soldier fulfilling his office by punishing the wicked, killing the wicked, and creating so much misery, it seems an un-Christian work completely contrary to Christian love. But when I think of how it protects the good and keeps and preserves wife and child, house and farm, property, and honor and peace, then I see how precious and godly this work is; and I observe that it amputates a leg or a hand, so that the whole body may not perish. For if the sword were not on guard to preserve peace, everything in the world would be ruined because of lack of peace.[48]

While on the surface it would appear that a soldier engages in acts that many would not view as acts of love, for Luther, it is within the requirements of a soldier's vocation that we see love in action. As soldiers carry out their duty of protecting their nation and securing the peace, they are called to love and serve their fellow citizens by putting their lives on the line. While in their personal lives, they are called to love their enemy, however, in their vocation as soldiers they are called to "bear the sword."[49] With that comes actions that are necessary to defend the lives of their fellow citizens of the nation they are sworn to protect.

Our callings in our various stations of life, according to Luther, are designed by God to elicit service to others—married persons to each other, rulers to their subjects, etc.[50] However, what transforms vocation from mere service compelled by the work of the law to a free service to all is Christian love. Wingren notes this power of God's love working in the believer's vocation when he writes, "The variable element is love, which can freely go its way since it is God. The love of the new man, which shapes his 'use' of his office, is a form of God's new creation in the world."[51] In his book *The Spirituality of the Cross*, Veith explains that when we grow in faith by the justifying love of Christ, it is the work of the Holy Spirit in the new man that not only fills one's life with his love but also flows out in love and service to our neighbor.[52] In this way service to a neighbor is freely given from within, rather than compelled from without.

48. Luther, "Whether Soldiers," 218–19.
49. Veith, *God at Work*, 9.
50. Wingren, *Luther on Vocation*, 125.
51. Wingren, *Luther on Vocation*, 150.
52. Veith, *Spirituality of the Cross*, 77.

Luther captures this idea of a believer's calling being motivated by love for one's neighbor, rather than by obligation to the law, when he clearly explains,

> Behold, from faith thus flow forth love and joy in the Lord, and from love a joyful, willing, and free mind that serves one's neighbor willingly and takes no account of gratitude or ingratitude, of praise or blame, of gain or loss. For a man does not serve that he may put men under obligations. He does not distinguish between friends and enemies or anticipate their thankfulness or unthankfulness, but he most freely and most willingly spends himself and all that he has, whether he wastes all on the thankless or whether he gains reward.[53]

This freedom that comes by faith fills believers with joy as they live their earthly vocations for others. They are free from having to appease God with their good works according to the demand of the law. In turn, this frees them to love and serve their neighbor with true joy, expecting nothing in return because they are satisfied with "the fullness of wealth of his faith."[54] As water flows into a lake and out once again to make it fresh, so the living water of Christ's love naturally flows out from believers as they love their neighbor in their various stations of life.

Distinction between Believers and Non-Believers

An important distinction that needs to be made is the difference between believers and non-believers when it comes to Luther's understanding of vocation. Wingren highlights this difference when he writes, "Luther does not use Beruf or vocatio in reference to the work of a non-Christian. All have station (Stand) and office; but Beruf is the Christian's earthly or spiritual work."[55] Specifically, while believers and non-believers alike all have stations or offices, it is believers called and enlightened by the gospel who have true vocations in life. This teaching of Luther's runs counter to the despiritualized understanding of vocation in our culture today. In spite of this important distinction, we can still affirm how God works through

---

53. Luther, "Freedom of a Christian," 619.
54. Lull, *Luther's Basic Theological Writings*, 617.
55. Wingren, *Luther on Vocation*, 2.

the stations and areas of responsibilities of unbelievers, which, as Wingren stresses, function the same outwardly as the vocations of believers.[56]

The key difference between non-believers and believers, in terms of living out their areas of responsibilities, is not the outward performance of their stations but the internal motivation of their hearts.[57] Luther preaches on the internal motivation for the believer in his "Gospel for the Early Christmas Service" when he proclaims:

> For being a Christian does not consist in external conduct, neither does it change anyone according to his external position; rather it changes him according to the inner disposition, that is to say, it provides a different heart, a different disposition, will, and mind which do the works which another person does without such a disposition and will. For a Christian knows that it all depends upon faith; for this reason he walks, stands, eats, drinks, dresses, works, and lives as any ordinary person in his calling, so that one does not become aware of his Christianity, as Christ says in Luke 17 [vv. 20–21]: "The kingdom of God does not come in an external manner and one cannot say, 'Lo, here and there,' but the kingdom of God is within you."[58]

Externally there is virtually no difference in the appearance and behavior of non-believers and believers in fulfilling the responsibilities of one's station. The difference is an internal one. For the non-believer, the law works in one's station, compelling their behavior outwardly regardless of the condition of their heart. However, for the believer, it is the gospel that renews their heart and fills it with love for their neighbor, making their service a joy-filled one.[59]

What transforms everything for the believer, in terms of their stations in life, is faith. Faith transforms a station into a true calling. Faith is the power of God that creates a willing heart of love and service for one's neighbor. Faith allows one's vocation to be carried out aligned to God's purpose and design.[60] Luther expounds on the transforming power of faith in his exposition of 1 Cor 7 when he states,

---

56. Veith, *Working for Our Neighbor*, 6.
57. Veith, *Working for Our Neighbor*, 6.
58. Luther, "Early Christmas Service," 214.
59. Wingren, *Luther on Vocation*, 47.
60. Wingren, *Luther on Vocation*, 71.

> When faith leads to action in outward affairs, that which takes place is spiritual in the midst of the carnal. Everything that our bodies do, the external and carnal, is and is called spiritual behavior, if God's Word is added to it and it is done in faith. There is therefore nothing which is so bodily, carnal, and external that it does not become spiritual when it is done in the Word of God and faith.[61]

As a result of faith, believers see their ordinary responsibilities in life with new spiritual significance.[62] And by the Spirit's working, believers can now rejoice in their vocations as true callings from God.[63]

There has been a significant amount of time and energy spent on increasing employee engagement and satisfaction in the workplace here in the US and around the world. Gallup®[64] has consistently found that only one third of all employees in the US are engaged in the workplace, leaving two thirds disengaged or actively disengaged.[65] Even so, Barna has found that more than three fourths of Christians in the workplace are either very (35 percent) or somewhat (39 percent) satisfied with their current job, with only 5 percent being very unsatisfied. Also, a majority of believers say that their "unique strengths, talents, and abilities" are being utilized in their present job (42 percent "strongly agree," 43 percent "somewhat agree").[66] The question might be asked, "What is the difference?" When Luther's teaching on vocation is taken into consideration, faith may be one of the most significant indicators of workplace engagement and satisfaction.

IT'S ALL ABOUT RELATIONSHIPS

When all things are considered, at a foundational level, life is all about relationships—the relationship one has with oneself, the relationship one has with others, the relationship one has with both the challenges and opportunities in life, and, ultimately, the relationship one has with God. This life was intended by God to be made up of a network of interdependent

---

61. Wingren, *Luther on Vocation*, 70.
62. Veith, *God at Work*, 61.
63. Wingren, *Luther on Vocation*, 44.
64. Gallup®, CliftonStrengths® and the CliftonStrengths 34 Themes of Talent are trademarks of Gallup, Inc. All rights reserved.
65. Gallup, *State of the American*, 17.
66. Barna, *Christians at Work*, 31.

relationships where people are giving and receiving from one another in life. That is the picture that Luther paints throughout in his teaching of vocation. Veith describes Luther's view of interdependence in the following way, "The picture is of a vast, complex network of human beings with different talents and abilities. Each serves the other. Each is served by others. . . . Because of the centrality of love, we are to depend on other human beings and, ultimately and through them, on God."[67] Love and service to one's neighbor is the heart and soul of God's design, purpose, and will for life.

Unfortunately, this life of interdependency is not the life many experience today. Our American culture encourages people to look out for number one and to be self-dependent. As a nation we are self-centered and self-obsessed because of our sinfulness. As a result, we neither love God or love our neighbor as we search for our own meaning and significance in life.[68] This by-product of not only sin but both the utilitarian and expressive individualism we see in our culture today, is leading to an increase in loneliness and isolation.[69] Jean Twenge, in her book *Generation Me*, highlights this shift that has happened in our culture when she writes, "One study found that in 1985, the average American had three people with whom he or she could 'discuss important matters'; by 2004, that number had shrunk to zero. Our social contacts are slight compared to those enjoyed by earlier generations."[70] While many young people today may have multiple "friends" on Facebook and other social media platforms, this doesn't necessarily translate into the ability to create healthy relationships in real life.

The antidote for this me-ism, and subsequent loneliness and isolation many are experiencing in our culture today, is Luther's teaching on vocation. As believers live out their calling in Christ in their various stations in life, they find themselves in a matrix of multiple relationships. Wingren locates the believer amid this matrix when he writes,

> Man in his vocation is in the earthly kingdom hoping for the heavenly kingdom, which comes to him here through the gospel, but which will not be fully revealed in power until after death. Thus he stands between heaven and earth. But he also stands between

---

67. Veith, *Spirituality of the Cross*, 76.
68. Benne, *Ordinary Saints*, 38–39.
69. Kuehne, *Sex in the iWorld*, 77.
70. Twenge, *Generation Me*, 150.

> God and the devil. His vocation is one of the situations in which he chooses sides in the combat between God and Satan.[71]

There is a sort of a dualism that exists as Luther sees man pinpointed between these various relationships, suspended between heaven and earth and pulled between God and the evil one.[72]

The first and primary relationship that believers stand between is the realm of heaven and the realm of earth. The believer lives as a dual-citizen in both of these realms.[73] As a result, according to Luther, we have a double vocation—a spiritual one in heaven as a result of our faith, as well as a baptismal identity and an external one on earth, which is also divine.[74] God governs in both realms distinctly, earth by his law and heaven by his gospel.[75] Luther explains these different ways by which God rules when he explains, "We set forth two worlds, as it were, one of them heavenly and the other earthly. Into these we place these Two Kinds of Righteousness, which are distinct and separated from each other."[76] As I will expand upon in further detail later, we hear from Luther that there are Two Kinds of Righteousness, or ways of being right, in one's relationship with God and one's neighbor. The first comes by faith through the gospel, whereby a believer's conscience is caught up into the realm of heaven and rests in Christ. The second comes from the demands of the law expressed in stations in life, whereby in love, a believer descends into the realm of earth to serve their neighbor.[77]

The other relationship that believers stand between is the pull between the reign of God and the reign of Satan in their hearts as they live out their vocation in their stations of life. Luther addresses this tug-of-war when he explains,

> On the other hand in relation to God, or in matters pertaining to salvation or damnation, a man has no free choice, but is a captive, subject and slave either of the will of God or the will of Satan.[78]

---

71. Wingren, *Luther on Vocation*, xi.
72. Wingren, *Luther on Vocation*, 162.
73. Siemon-Netto, "Vocation vs. Narcissus," 8.
74. Froehlich, "Luther on Vocation," 202–3.
75. Froehlich, "Luther on Vocation," 202–3.
76. Luther, "Lectures on Galatians," 8.
77. Luther, "Freedom of a Christian," 623.
78. Luther, "Career of the Reformer III," 70.

From Luther's perspective, there is no unilateral choice or freedom when it comes to one's salvation. Either one is in the hand of God, or one is in the hand of the evil one. We are never free agents—even in our vocations as believers. As will be explained later in the section on "God and Satan," either one is living out their calling for God's glory as they serve their neighbor, or one is sinning against their vocation by living for ourselves. And by doing so in the latter, individuals unwittingly fulfill the purposes of the devil as Peter did in his encounter with Jesus in Matt 16:23. It is here in relationship between heaven and earth, as well as the pull between God and Satan, that believers live that sinner/saint reality (*simul justus et peccator*) that defines so accurately the life and calling of a Christian.

Vertical Calling in Heaven

The first and primary relationship that a believer has that defines their person and empowers them for living out their vocation in life is their vertical relationship with God through Christ. This is the believer's relationship with the realm of heaven. Luther discusses in his work "Two Kinds of Righteousness" this relationship that makes us right with God, as he explains,

> There are two kinds of Christian righteousness, just as man's sin is of two kinds. . . . The first is alien righteousness, that is the righteousness of another, instilled from without. This is the righteousness of Christ by which he justifies through faith, as it is written in 1 Cor. 19:30: "Whom God made our wisdom, our righteousness and sanctification and redemption."[79]

This "alien righteousness" is also known theologically as "passive righteousness" because it is received passively without any work, effort, or merit on our own.[80] This is the righteousness that transformed Luther as he read Romans. It is a righteousness that comes by faith in Jesus, apart from the law, in which we "are all justified freely by his grace through the redemption that came by Christ Jesus" (Rom 3:24 NIV).

The vertical relationship a believer has with Christ is established solely by God's working through the Word and Sacraments, the means by which we receive his undeserved grace that produces faith. It's not about who we are and what we have done. It is instead about who Jesus is and what he has

---

79. Luther, "Two Kinds," 155.
80. Luther, "Lectures on Galatians," 8.

done for us. It's all Jesus all the time. As we hear from Paul in Eph 2:8–9 (ESV), "For by grace you have been saved through faith. And this is not your own doing; it is the gift of God, not a result of works, so that no one may boast." Luther explains how we receive this righteousness and grace as a gift through faith from God in our relationship with him when he states,

> This righteousness, then, is given to men in baptism and whenever they are truly repentant. Therefore a man can with confidence boast in Christ and say: "Mine are Christ's living, doing, and speaking, his suffering and dying, mine as much as if I had lived, done, spoken, suffered, and died as he did."[81]

For Luther it is in baptism that God unites us into the death and resurrection of Jesus (Rom 6:3–6). Jesus' death becomes our death and his life becomes our life. Our old self dies, and we are given a new baptismal identity in Christ.

This righteousness from God given in baptism frees believers from the temptation to look to their good works in life in order to try to earn God's favor. As Benne states, "The Christian life begins and ends in the grace of God. That is, we are not finally justified before God by how well we, in fact, perform our callings."[82] We are all tempted to invert what we do in our horizontal stations of life and use it to try to earn God's favor in our vertical relationship with him. Luther counters this impulse by pointing believers to where God's favor can be found, "So all these are called simply good and holy works. Nevertheless none of these orders is a way to salvation. There is only one way, which is above all these, namely faith in Jesus Christ."[83] Our identity and righteousness before God is now in Christ alone! This truth frees believers from the need to look to their vocation in life to define their relationship before God. As a result, in his work "The Freedom of the Christian," Luther proclaims that before God, in the believer's vertical relationship through Christ, "A Christian is a perfectly free lord of all, subject to none."[84]

When it comes to believers living out their calling in Christ in their various stations of life, it is essential to remember that our being always precedes our doing.[85] Today, so many are tempted to look at what they

---

81. Luther, "Two Kinds," 155.
82. Benne, *Ordinary Saints*, 120.
83. Wingren, *Luther on Vocation*, 64.
84. Luther, "Freedom of a Christian," 596.
85. Benne, *Ordinary Saints*, 55.

accomplish or how well they perform as the basis for their identity in life. An example of this temptation is where Gen Z looks to for their ultimate sense of identity. According to Barna Group, 43 percent look to their professional and educational achievement for their sense of identity, while only 34 percent look to faith for their identity.[86] This happened in my story during my wilderness experience in ministry. I didn't realize how much my ultimate sense of identity had become so wrapped up in being a pastor, rather than in Christ. Benne reminds believers how to keep a proper sense of their true identity as they seek to live out their callings in life, "But the indicative—you are affirmed, loved, forgiven—precedes the imperative: therefore, go and do the will of your Father who is in heaven."[87]

Horizontal Calling on Earth

The second, yet no less significant, relationship a believer has is their horizontal vocation with their fellow neighbors in their various stations of life. This is the believer's relationship with the realm of earth. Again, in his work "Two Kinds of Righteousness," Luther continues to explore the nature of righteousness when he discusses this relationship that makes believers right with their fellow man:

> The second kind of righteousness is our proper righteousness, not because we alone work it, but because we work with that first and alien righteousness. This is that manner of life spent profitably in good works, in the first place, in slaying the flesh and crucifying the desires with respect to the self, of which we read in Gal 5 (:24): "And those who belong to Christ Jesus have crucified the flesh with its passions and desires." In the second place, this righteousness consists in love to one's neighbor, and in the third place, in meekness and fear toward God.[88]

This "proper" righteousness that Luther describes is also known theologically in Lutheran circles as "civic" righteousness.[89] Within Luther's teaching on vocation, it is this righteousness that guides and directs any relationship believers have on the horizontal plane of life in their various areas of

---

86. Barna Group and Impact 360, *Gen Z*, 41.
87. Benne, *Ordinary Saints*, 28.
88. Luther, "Two Kinds," 157.
89. Luther, "Lectures on Galatians," 6.

responsibility.⁹⁰ It calls believers to die to self that they may be born in love for one's neighbor.⁹¹ All this as they seek to bring glory to God by letting their light shine through their good works in service to others (Matt 5:16).

Believers need to remember that God does not just rule in his spiritual realm, but his earthly realm as well.⁹² Though, he does so in a different way. God governs heaven by the gospel, and he governs earth by the law working through the various stations and offices of believers and unbelievers alike.⁹³ A mystery of vocation is that God works in and through the callings of believers and their stations in life. Wingren expresses this thought when he states, "The good that man does on earth is God's creation, and it is to be directed toward his neighbor."⁹⁴ As will be explored more in depth, vocation is ultimately God's work, reaching down, through the believer for the care of humanity.⁹⁵ This vision of vocation can infuse one's ordinary life with greater God-given meaning and purpose.

So, what is the purpose of our vocations as believers? Why does God call us and place us in our areas of responsibilities that we have in life? For Luther, it is about this one simple idea—vocation is all about loving and serving one's neighbors.⁹⁶ Gustaf Wingren, in perhaps his most significant quote on his evaluation of Luther's theological instruction on the topic of vocation, expresses it this way:

> In heaven, before God, vocation has as little to contribute as do good works. Good works and vocation (love) exist for the earth and one's neighbor, not for eternity and God. God does not need our good works, but our neighbor does.⁹⁷

Again, the good works believers trust in for salvation are Jesus' good works. This good news frees them to use their good works in service to their neighbor as they carry out their areas of responsibility in life. Luther echoes this truth regarding the nature of good works in discussing the meaning of the fourth commandment in his "Large Catechism," "In God's sight it is

---

90. Wingren, *Luther on Vocation*, 5.
91. Luther, "Two Kinds," 158.
92. Veith, *God at Work*, 29–30.
93. Wingren, *Luther on Vocation*, 93.
94. Wingren, *Luther on Vocation*, 18.
95. Wingren, *Luther on Vocation*, 11.
96. Veith, *God at Work*, 39–40.
97. Wingren, *Luther on Vocation*, 10.

actually faith that makes a person holy, it alone serves God, while our works serve people."[98] Believers have been given all they need for salvation. It is their neighbor who is in need.[99] Luther captures this servant posture of the believer for their neighbor in their horizontal relationships in life when he states, "A Christian is a perfectly dutiful servant of all, subject to all."[100]

There is a place for good works in the life of believers. Many Lutheran Christians struggle with this notion of good works because of the abuse of many to try to earn salvation in the monastery before the Reformation. However, if one keeps Luther's theological framework of alien and proper righteousness separate, good works in service to one's neighbor can be celebrated within the context of vocation. In fact, we were created for good works. Paul states this in Eph 2:10 (ESV) when he writes, "For we are his workmanship, created in Christ Jesus for good works, which God prepared beforehand, that we should walk in them." The good works believers were created and now redeemed to do in a general sense is to love and serve their neighbor in their various stations of life. Luther provides a practical guide for believers to begin to love and serve their neighbor, in their various areas of responsibility, in the table of duties, contained within his *Small Catechism*.[101]

Based on what Paul says in Eph 2:10, each believer will also do good works of loving and serving their neighbor that will be unique to that person, based on their God-given gifts and talents. In his commentary on Genesis, Luther encourages his readers to use their unique talents and gifts in their daily vocations when he writes, "And this is why God has given man reason, perception, and strength. Use these as means and gifts of God."[102] Discerning one's vocation involves recognizing one's God-given talents and abilities, as well as identifying God-given opportunities to use them to serve others.[103] Veith notes this when he writes, "These are valued as gifts of God, who creates and equips each person in a different way for the calling He has in mind for that person's life."[104] It is Benne who suggests a three-step process to help believers to gain awareness of the unique good works

---

98. Luther, "Large Catechism," 406.
99. Wingren, *Luther on Vocation*, 108–9.
100. Luther, "Freedom of a Christian," 596.
101. Luther, *Luther's Small Catechism*, 33–38.
102. Luther, "Lectures on Genesis," 95.
103. Veith, *God at Work*, 7.
104. Veith, *God at Work*, 21.

they are called to do in service to others. This process involves increasing awareness of one's God-given talents and gifts, assessing opportunities to serve others, and finally discerning, with the help of the Holy Spirit, where the intersection is between one's capacities and the world's needs.[105]

However, an important question to address is, what is the catalyst that prompts love and good works within the life of the believer as they live their vocation in their horizontal relationships of life? What makes a believer's service to their neighbor not just a mere outward submitting of their actions in the flesh but a joy-filled response of the heart? Luther answers these questions when he explains,

> This righteousness is the product of the righteousness of the first type, actually its fruit and consequence, for we read in Gal 5 (:22): "But the fruit of the spirit (i.e., of a spiritual man, whose very existence depends on faith in Christ) is love, joy, peace, patience, kindness, goodness, faithfulness, gentleness, self-control."[106]

It is the righteousness of faith that produces the fruit of faith—love. Love born of faith comes down from the realm of heaven and breaks into the realm of the earth in the heart of believers, as God's love did in the incarnation of Jesus.[107] This love overflows from the heart of the believer and moves them to love and serve their neighbor. It prompts believers to ask the following questions, that Veith puts forth, as they think about their vocation in life: "How does my calling serve my neighbor? Who are my neighbors in my particular vocation, and how can I serve them with the love of God?"[108] The answer to these questions will be unique for each individual given their God-given talents and gifts, as well as the needs of their neighbors that God has placed in their life to serve.

The Reign of God and Satan

Besides the dichotomy between the relationship of the realm of heaven and the realm of earth, there is a second relationship that must be taken seriously as believers seek to live out their vocation. That is the relationship between the kingdom or reign of God versus the kingdom or reign of Satan.

---

105. Benne, *Ordinary Saints*, 105.
106. Luther, "Two Kinds," 158.
107. Wingren, *Luther on Vocation*, 41.
108. Veith, *God at Work*, 40.

In his seminal work "Bondage of the Will" Luther discusses this conflict between God and the devil for the heart of humanity when he writes,

> For Christians know there are two kingdoms in the world, which are bitterly opposed to each other. In one of them Satan reigns, who is therefore called by Christ "the ruler of this world" (John 12:31) and by Paul "the god of this world" (II Cor. 4:4). . . . In the other Kingdom, Christ reigns, and his Kingdom ceaselessly resists and makes war on the kingdom of Satan. Into this Kingdom we are transferred, not by our own power but by the grace of God, by which we are set free from the present evil age and delivered from the dominion of darkness.[109]

Humanity stands in the middle of this struggle between the reign of God and the reign of the devil within the human heart.[110] It is within the areas of responsibility of each person that this battle is waged.[111] As Luther explains in his exposition of Ps 101, "The offices of princes and officials are divine and right, but those who are in them and use them are usually of the devil."[112] The stations and offices in this world are God's, but those who fill and exercise those areas of responsibility either are on God's side or Satan's side.[113] This has a major impact on how those stations are exercised, even for believers.

As mentioned before, there is a tug-of-war for the hearts of people, even believers seeking to live out their vocation in life. Either one is being used by God for good purposes, or one is being used by Satan for evil purposes. Luther notes this battle for the heart in his writing "An Open Letter Concerning the Hard Book against the Peasants" when he states,

> Who is lord of his own heart? Who can resist the devil and the flesh? Indeed, it is not possible for us to ward off the lightest sin, for the Scriptures say that we are captives of the devil, as though he were our prince and god, so that we have to do what he wills and what he puts into our hearts [2 Tim. 2:26]. There are some terrible stories to prove this. Ought such sins therefore go unpunished and

---

109. Luther, "Bondage of the Will, 1525," 218.
110. Wingren, *Luther on Vocation*, 145.
111. Wingren, *Luther on Vocation*, 141.
112. Luther, "Selected Psalms II," 212.
113. Wingren, *Luther on Vocation*, 85.

be thought right? Indeed not! It is our duty to call upon God for help and to resist sin and wrong."[114]

It is through the gospel that God rescues us from the reign of the evil one, creating faith in the heart that overflows with love for our neighbor.[115] However, as Luther explained, there is a continuing battle that goes on in the heart of believers after they are saved to resist the evil one and his purposes. In those times that believers, either knowingly or unknowingly, allow Satan to have his way in their hearts as they love themselves rather than their neighbor, God uses the law to compel the flesh and the gospel to draw them back to his heart.[116]

While there are obvious activities that are contrary to God's will, where Satan works most often is in his attempt to tempt believers to misuse and sin against their areas of responsibilities in life. As Wingren notes, "Temptation in vocation is the devil's attempt to get man out of his vocation."[117] Each station and office in life has its own distinctive temptation.[118] Be it negligence, indifference, or idleness—all these are used by the devil to move a believer away from God's purpose of serving one's neighbor to serving one's self instead.[119] Satan also tempts believers to think what they do in their stations in the realm of earth has eternal rewards in the realm of heaven, trying to steal away faith or receptivity to God.[120]

To counter what Wingren calls a "satanic transformation" of our vocation, God has given believers two powerful tools in which to do battle against the evil one—the Word and prayer.[121] In regard to the power of the Word being used against Satan, Luther states, "Only the Word uncovers him, so that he cannot hide himself."[122] God's Word reveals the truth about the devil's attempts to pull us away from our calling of faith in God and our calling of love to neighbor. The Word also reveals how we should live out our vocation in our relationship with our neighbors in our various areas

---

114. Luther, "Christian in Society III," 77.
115. Wingren, *Luther on Vocation*, 14.
116. Wingren *Luther on Vocation*, 79.
117. Wingren, *Luther on Vocation*, 121.
118. Veith, *God at Work*, 135.
119. Wingren, *Luther on Vocation*, 100.
120. Wingren, *Luther on Vocation*, 139.
121. Wingren, *Luther on Vocation*, 96.
122. Wingren, *Luther on Vocation*, 122.

of responsibility in life.¹²³ In regards to the power of prayer in our battle against the enemy, Wingren states, "To pray is to depart from the devil's power, in which man stands over against God, and to enter into the power of God, in which man stands over against the devil."¹²⁴ Prayer, which is an act of faith, moves the believer from the hand of Satan to the hand of God for noble use in their vocation once again.¹²⁵

Law and Gospel

The last relationship believers need to navigate as they live out their vocation in Christ, in their stations and offices in life, is the Law and the Gospel. As Luther notes in "The Freedom of a Christian," one can separate all of Scripture into these two parts—"commandments," which is the Law of God, and "promises," which is the Gospel of God in Christ.¹²⁶ Luther stresses the importance of the distinction of these two aspects of God's Word when he writes,

> The knowledge of this topic, the distinction between the Law and the Gospel, is necessary to the highest degree; for it contains a summary of all Christian doctrine. Therefore let everyone learn diligently how to distinguish the Law from the Gospel, not only in words but in feeling and in experience; that is, let him distinguish well between these two in his heart and in his conscience.... But in a matter apart from conscience, when outward duties must be performed, then, whether you are a preacher, a magistrate, a husband, a teacher, a pupil, etc., this is no time to listen to the Gospel. You must listen to the Law and follow your vocation. Thus the Law remains in the valley with the ass, and the Gospel remains with Isaac on the mountain.¹²⁷

The Law condemns, but the Gospel saves. Besides our conscience with God, the Law governs the old nature when it comes to obligations and duties regarding our neighbors in our vocation on earth. The Gospel, on the other hand, governs the new nature regarding our relationship with God through our calling of faith in Christ. Vocation is of the Law, but the Gospel

---

123. Wingren, *Luther on Vocation*, 123.
124. Wingren, *Luther on Vocation*, 83.
125. Wingren, *Luther on Vocation*, 83.
126. Luther, "Freedom of a Christian," 600.
127. Luther, "Lectures on Galatians," 117.

transforms the vocation of believers with freedom in regard to love and service to their neighbor.[128]

The Law functions, or is used by God, in two ways. The first function of the Law is civil, which governs our earthly affairs of this life on earth, and the second function of the Law is spiritual, which governs our conscience before God.[129] It is this first, or civil, function of the Law where Luther located vocation in the horizontal relationships of life.[130] Luther expounds further on this first use of the Law when he explains,

> For the Law was given for two uses. The first is to restrain those who are uncivilized and wicked. In this sense the statement, "He who does these things shall live by them," is a political statement. It means: If a man obeys the magistrate outwardly and in the civil realm, he will avoid punishment and death. The civil magistrate has no right to impose punishments upon him or to execute him but permits him to live with impunity. This is the civil use of the Law, which is valid for the restraint of the uncivilized.[131]

This is the Law as it is used by God as a curb to those who would do evil and to keep society orderly through earthly authorities.[132] It shows believers and unbelievers alike what is required of them in their stations in life.[133] Through this civil functioning of God's Law, his will and purpose for his good creation are expressed, and our relationships in our various areas of responsibilities in life are ordered.[134] It is also how God provides for the world, and people are cared for through vocation.[135] The problem is that Satan tempts believers to try to use this first function of the Law on earth to justify themselves before God in heaven.[136]

The second function of the Law that governs our conscience before God is also known as the theological use.[137] When believers are tempted to invert their civic righteousness in their areas of responsibility in life, it

---

128. Wingren, *Luther on Vocation*, 66.
129. Wingren, *Luther on Vocation*, 61.
130. Kolden, *Christian's Calling*, 24–25.
131. Luther, "Lectures on Galatians," 274–75.
132. Wingren, *Luther on Vocation*, 60.
133. Wingren, *Luther on Vocation*, 107.
134. Kolden, "Luther on Vocation," 385–86.
135. Kolden, *Christian's Calling*, 32.
136. Wingren, *Luther on Vocation*, 169.
137. Luther, "Lectures on Galatians," 309.

is this primary function of the Law that shows them their shortcomings before God's righteous requirements. Luther describes this functioning of the Law when he notes:

> Although the commandments teach things that are good, the things taught are not done as soon as they are taught, for the commandments show us what we ought to do but do not give us the power to do it. They are intended to teach man to know himself, that through them he may recognize his inability to do good and may despair of his own ability.[138]

The theological use of the Law is to show us our sins and our need for a savior. Often, we think more highly of ourselves than we ought to as humans. The second function of the Law serves as a mirror, showing our fallen nature—showing how much our lives are curved in on ourselves, at the exclusion of loving our neighbor as well as God expects, let alone loving him as we ought to with all of ourselves.[139] In his *Small Catechism* Luther instructs believers, convicted of their shortcomings before neighbor and God, to confess their sins:

> Consider your place in life [stations] according to the Ten Commandments: Are you a father, mother, son, daughter, husband, wife, or worker? Have you been disobedient, unfaithful, or lazy? Have you been hot-tempered, rude, or quarrelsome? Have you hurt someone in your words or deeds? Have you stolen, been negligent, wasted anything, or done any harm?[140]

In light of the Ten Commandments, Luther calls believers to look in the mirror of the second function of the Law to see how they may have failed to love and serve their neighbor in their various areas of responsibility. Any sin against one's neighbor is a sin against one's calling in life.[141]

Once the second function of the Law has had its way within the heart of man and shown them that their earthly righteousness does not earn God's righteousness, they are ready for the Gospel. The Gospel is the good news of what Jesus has done on behalf of humanity through his life, death, and resurrection that humanity could not do for itself. Luther explains the effect of the Gospel on the human heart when he writes,

---

138. Luther, "Freedom of a Christian," 600.
139. Luther, "Lectures on Romans," 345.
140. Luther, *Luther's Small Catechism*, 25.
141. Veith, *God at Work*, 135.

> The Word is the Gospel of God concerning his Son, who was made flesh, suffered, rose from the dead, and was glorified through the Spirit who sanctifies. To preach Christ means to free the soul, make it righteous, set it free, and save it, provided it believes the preaching.[142]

Through the effect of the Gospel, believers are forgiven and saved. They also receive Christ's righteousness and are now free from the need to justify themselves before God. There is now freedom for the believer in terms of their actions regarding their relationship with their neighbors in their vocation.[143] The believer's vocation to love one's neighbor is not abolished; it is redefined and filled with renewed purpose.[144] Faith in the heart and the call to love and serve one's neighbor are now aligned.[145] The grace that the believer received through the work of the Gospel by faith makes them eager to want to love and serve their neighbor with fresh enthusiasm by the working of the Spirit.[146]

STATIONS OF LIFE

As Luther envisioned the vocation of believers loving and serving their neighbors, he taught that there were specific stations or offices in the horizontal plane of life where these activities were to be located. Wingren notes that in his *Vom Abendmahl Christi*, Luther divides these areas of responsibility into three "holy orders and true institutions, established by God: the office of the ministry, marriage, and earthly government."[147] For Luther these are all part of God's continuing work of creation and can be understood as the "orders of creation."[148] Over time the responsibilities of marriage and work were separated due to economic and societal changes. As a result these two are often in conflict with each other rather than integrated, like in Luther's day.[149] Today it can be understood that there are four distinct stations that believers can occupy—family, work, society/state, and

---

142. Luther, "Freedom of a Christian," 598.
143. Wingren, *Luther on Vocation*, 62.
144. Wingren, *Luther on Vocation*, 66.
145. Wingren, *Luther on Vocation*, 73.
146. Paustian, "Unleashing Our Calling," 11–12.
147. Wingren, *Luther on Vocation*, 63.
148. Benne, *Ordinary Saints*, 63.
149. Veith, *Working for Our Neighbor*, 6.

the Church.[150] Believers can hold a number of these stations all at once.[151] Even within these four unique stations, there are various offices that a believer can hold as well. For example, within the station of family, one can be a daughter, a wife, and a mother all at one time—each with their unique responsibilities.

Calling in the Church

A unique station that believers are called to stands at the intersection of heaven and earth—that is the Church. Even though it is heavenly, it doesn't lose its earthly quality as it is made up of people who, at the same time, are sinners and saints.[152] Luther describes how God creates the Church when he explains in his *Small Catechism*, "In the same way He calls, gathers, enlightens, and sanctifies the whole Christian church on earth, and keeps it with Jesus Christ in the one true faith."[153] Believers are called out from the world through the preaching of the Word and the administration of the Sacraments (Baptism and the Lord's Supper) where Jesus is present, creating faith in the heart.[154] Regarding the significance of this justifying and sanctifying work of God to vocation in the rest of life, Benne writes, "Among all the callings of the Christian, the church is a very special one because it conveys our fundamental identity, provides our worldview, and provides the rationale for all other callings."[155] This calling serves as the lens for how a believer is to see themselves, others, and the world around them.

Within the Church, Jesus has given the Office of the Keys, which is the ministry of forgiving and binding sin.[156] God calls some believers to a distinct office within the Church to exercise this gift of Christ—the pastoral office. Luther describes the blessing and value of this vocation located specifically within the Church to believers when he states,

> He paid clearly that men might everywhere have this office of preaching, baptizing, loosing, binding, giving the sacrament,

---

150. Benne, *Ordinary Saints*, 62.
151. Wingren, *Luther on Vocation*, 5.
152. Benne, *Ordinary Saints*, 204.
153. Luther, *Luther's Small Catechism*, 15.
154. Veith, *God at Work*, 122.
155. Benne, *Ordinary Saints*, 217.
156. Luther, *Luther's Small Catechism*, 27.

> comforting, warning, and exhorting with God's word, and whatever else belongs to the pastoral office. For this office not only helps to further and sustain this temporal life and all the worldly estates, but it also gives eternal life and delivers from sin, and death, which is its proper and chief work. Indeed, it is only because of the spiritual estate that the world stands and abides at all; if it were not for this estate, the world would long since have gone down to destruction.[157]

As has been discussed before, the pastoral office or service of any professional church worker is no greater than that of an accountant or doctor or construction worker. Before God, all vocations stand as equal and are holy. Nevertheless, it is a distinct office because through its exercise, spiritual gifts are given to strengthen believers for life and faith in their vocations.[158] Here believers are refreshed, renewed, equipped, and empowered by Christ through those who work in full-time ministry for their service to their neighbor the rest of the week.

In both 1 Cor 12 and Eph 4, the apostle Paul calls the Church, the body of Christ. As such, believers are a part of the body, each with their unique gifts and talents to offer. Though not everyone is called to full-time ministry, that does not mean that they can't contribute to the ministry of a local congregation with their gifts, and be there to love and serve their neighbor.[159] While this is a great blessing to the mission of God's Church, believers need to remember that serving God also takes place in the rest of their stations of life—family, work, society. As Veith reminds believers, "The Christian faith is to be lived out not primarily in the activities of the church—which is the realm of the gospel, where one receives the forgiveness of sins—but in vocation."[160] Believers have daily opportunities to love and serve their neighbors in their other stations in life. They should not be taken away from those too much by the Church. There they also have the chance to share the good news of Christ with those who have never heard as they serve as his witnesses. As the body of Christ, collectively and individually a part of it, believers, very literally, are the presence of Jesus in our world today. They are his feet that go, they are his hands that reach, and

---

157. Luther, "Sermon on Keeping Children," 222.
158. Veith, *God at Work*, 123.
159. Paustian, "Unleashing Our Calling," 16.
160. Veith, *Working for Our Neighbor*, 28–29.

they are his voice that speaks to those God has called them to neighbor in their various areas of responsibility each day.

Calling in the Family

The second station that believers are called to in the horizontal plane of life is their vocation in the family. When Luther was developing his teaching on vocation, it was the family, and more specifically, marriage, that he addressed the most. For him, it is foundational because it was established in the beginning at creation and is part of God's ongoing creative work through the procreation of children.[161] Luther also saw the family as foundational for vocation in the other orders of creation, because from the authority of fathers and mothers grew civil, societal, and, even, spiritual authority.[162] Thus, it is the basis for the notion of citizenship as well as service to one's neighbor.

Vocation in the family begins with the relationship between husbands and wives. Counter to the view of marriage and sex before the Reformation, Luther and the other reformers upheld marriage, the family, and sex as true blessings from God.[163] The purpose of marriage, like Luther's vision for vocation overall, is for husbands and wives to love and serve each other.[164] And, within the bounds of this committed relationship, to start a family if God so willed. If a husband and wife were blessed to have children, then as father and mother they would be called, as Luther so vividly explains in his work "The Estate of Marriage," to love and serve their offspring:

> Now you tell me, when a father goes ahead and washes diapers or performs some other mean task for his child, and someone ridicules him as an effeminate fool—though that father is acting in the spirit just described and in Christian faith—my dear fellow you tell me, which of the two is most keenly ridiculing the other? God, with all his angels and creatures, is smiling—not because that father is washing diapers, but because he is doing so in Christian faith. Those who sneer at him and see only the task but not the faith are ridiculing God with all his creatures, as the biggest fool

---

161. Kolden, "Luther on Vocation," 386–87.
162. Veith, *God at Work*, 78.
163. Veith, *God at Work*, 79.
164. Veith, *God at Work*, 80.

on earth. Indeed, they are only ridiculing themselves; with all their cleverness they are nothing but devil's fools.[165]

Here Luther uplifts even a father changing the diapers of a child as a holy act when done in faith, and the changing table serves as an altar to God. At this moment he is loving and serving his neighbor in the face of his child, as all parents are called to do in their vocation within families.

Besides caring for their children's physical needs, fathers and mothers are also to care for their children's spiritual needs. Not only are parents to raise their children in the faith in the church but they are also called to serve as "mini-pastors" in something like a "mini-church" within the family. This responsibility is perhaps the greatest way that parents can love and serve their children.[166] Luther reinforces this idea of the priestly role of parents with their children when he states,

> For it is the duty of father and mother—nay, for this very purpose they were made father and mother by God—to teach children and lead them to God not according to their own notion and their own religious persuasion but according to the command of God.[167]

This notion is reinforced in *Luther's Small Catechism*, which was intended not only to be used for educating the young within the Church but also for parents in teaching the faith at home. At the beginning of each section within Luther's catechism is this statement, "As the head of the family should teach them in a simple way to his household."[168] This charge by Luther was to encourage fathers and mothers to fulfill this spiritual vocation within their families as we hear in Prov 22:6 (ESV), "Train up a child in the way he should go; even when he is old he will not depart from it."

In the vocation of the family, it is not only spouses who are called to love and serve one another, and parents to love and serve their children, but it is also children who are called to love and serve their parents. Luther teaches about God's will for children in this regard when he reflects on the meaning of the fourth commandment in his "Large Catechism":

> "You are to honor your father and mother." God has given this walk of life, fatherhood and motherhood, a special position of honor, higher than that of any other walk of life under it. Not only

---

165. Luther, "Christian in Society II," 40–41.
166. Veith, *God at Work*, 85.
167. Plass, *What Luther Says*, 1021.
168. Luther, *Luther's Small Catechism*, 9.

has he commanded us to love parents but to honor them. In regard to brothers, sisters, and neighbors in general he commands nothing higher than that we love them.[169]

Luther's teaching on the believer's call to love and serve their neighbor no matter who they or even what their shortcomings may be in life is clearly highlighted in this quote. All of us are sinners in need of grace and forgiveness. But specifically, Luther teaches that children should honor their parents because of the special vocation they hold. He goes on to remind children of how their parents loved and served them by giving them life, nourished them, and even rescued them from their own filth a hundred times over.[170] As such, children should honor their parents by loving and serving them, as their parents have so often loved and served them.

Calling in the Workplace

There is a third station many believers are called to at some point in their life—the workplace. On the surface, work seems to be just merely a human endeavor providing goods and services for money in the global economic system.[171] However, through the eyes of faith, believers see that it is so much more. It is an interconnected network through which God provides for the needs of humanity through believers and unbelievers alike.[172] In today's culture, there is the temptation to either see work as a means simply to provide for one's daily needs (which can seem toilsome) or as a means for ultimate self-fulfillment (which leads to disappointment when expectations are not met).[173] However, through the eyes of faith, believers see that there is a higher purpose to their daily work. They have the privilege of participating in God's ongoing provision for the world as they love and serve their neighbors in and through the workplace.

No matter the work a believer does, be it lowly or great, it is all of equal value before God, because it is all for the purpose of making sure that one's neighbor is served.[174] Even the most menial of work from the

169. Luther, "Large Catechism," 400–401.
170. Luther, "Large Catechism," 404.
171. Benne, *Ordinary Saints*, 163.
172. Veith, *Working for Our Neighbor*, xvi.
173. Benne, *Ordinary Saints*, 166.
174. Benne, *Ordinary Saints*, 173.

world's perspective is filled with higher value when seen through the lens of Luther's teaching on vocation.[175] Luther invites believers to look around at their station of life and view their work from this perspective when he explains,

> To take a crude example again: If you are a manual laborer, you find that the Bible has been put into your workshop, into your hand, into your heart. It teaches and preaches how you should treat your neighbor. Just look at your tools—at your needle or thimble, your beer barrel, your goods, your scales or yardstick or measure—and you will read this statement inscribed on them. Everywhere you look, it stares at you. Nothing that you handle every day is so tiny that it does not continually tell you this, if you will only listen. Indeed, there is no shortage of preaching. You have as many preachers as you have transactions, goods, tools, and other equipment in your house and home. All this is continually crying out to you: "Friend, use me in your relations with your neighbor just as you would want your neighbor to use his property in his relations with you."[176]

This vision of Luther's regarding one's employment transforms the daily grind of work and what might be perceived as a dead-end job into something with divine significance. Whatever we do and wherever we work, through the eyes of faith we see that it is in some way, shape, or form serving our fellow man. And it is through the work of others that believers are loved and served as well.

This understanding of the vocation of believers in the workplace means that one must carry out their work mindful of how they are treating their co-workers, employees, and customers. In discussing the meaning of the seventh commandment, Luther, as he so many times does both, warns and encourages believers in how they should treat their neighbor in business when he writes,

> Let all people know, then, that it is their duty, on pain of God's displeasure, not to harm their neighbors, to take advantage of them, or defraud them by any faithless or underhanded business transaction. Much more than that, they are also obliged faithfully to protect their neighbors' property and to promote and further their interests, especially when they get money, wages, and provisions.[177]

---

175. Veith, *God at Work*, 74.
176. Luther, "Sermon on the Mount," 237.
177. Luther, "Large Catechism," 417.

While the Christian faith is not a religion of ethics, it does have ethical implications for how one carries out their vocation in the workplace in regard to how their neighbor is treated. Love and service to neighbor is the defining paradigm of how one's work and business practices should be viewed. Luther highlights the importance of this when discussing how merchants should approach their business practices when he states,

> First, among themselves the merchants have a common rule which is their chief maxim and the basis of all their sharp practices, where they say: "I may sell my goods as dear as I can." They think this is their right. Thus occasion is given for avarice, and every window and door to hell is opened. What else does it mean but this "I care nothing about my neighbor; so long as I have my profit and satisfy my greed, of what concern is it to me if it injures my neighbor in ten ways at once."[178]

This understanding of Luther's flies in the face of the ultimate maxim of our capitalist system that states, "Greed is good." While there is nothing inherently wrong with making a living in business, a believer is called to counter this temptation of profiting at the expense of the consumer by keeping a kingdom perspective that love and service to neighbor is God's will for one's vocation. Ultimately, this calls Christian business owners to greater social responsibility in their business practices.

Calling in Society

The last station believers are called to in their lives within the realm of earth is their vocation in society. For Luther, he primarily talked about this station in terms of the state or earthly governments. However, as Veith suggests, it might serve believers better to think of this station in terms of society or the more extensive networks of a culture or community.[179] This understanding can take into account a believer's vocation as a citizen of a nation, a resident of a city, or merely being a good neighbor in their apartment complex or cul-de-sac where they live.

According to Paul in Rom 13, God instituted the office of governing authorities, rulers, and the like to maintain order and peace in society. To them, he has given them the sword to punish evildoers. Ultimately, all

---

178. Luther, "Trade and Usury," 215.
179. Veith, *Working for Our Neighbor*, 7.

earthly authority is derived from God's authority. Echoing Paul's admonition in Romans, Luther encourages Christians to submit to governing authorities when he states,

> Nevertheless, although the Gospel does not subject us to the civil laws of Moses, it does not completely set us free from obedience to all political laws; but in this bodily life it subjects us to the laws of the state in which we live, and it commands everyone to obey his magistrate and his laws, "not only to avoid God's wrath but also for the sake of conscience" (1 Pet 2:13–14; Rom. 13:5).[180]

Luther calls believers to obey the laws of their land as part of living their vocation. While we have freedom in Christ, we are still bound in our vocation to live under the obligations of the nation in which we reside. And yet, we must remember that in those times that the laws of the state are not aligned with God's will, that we must heed the call of Peter, "We must obey God rather than men" (Acts 5:29 ESV).

Again, like other stations in the horizontal plane of life, believers have the opportunity to love and serve their neighbors by living their vocation within the larger society. One way in which believers can do this is through serving in government, as judges, in the military, or as firefighters or police officers. All these, as we have explored so far in Luther's teaching on vocation, are ways for believers to love and serve their neighbor. Believers, especially in democracies like ours here in the US, can engage in the responsibilities of citizenship by voting and political engagement. And perhaps the most significant way for believers to serve their neighbors is to get involved in a local non-profit and civic group that seeks the betterment of their community. However, serving one's neighbor also can be as simple as bringing some chicken soup to a neighbor who is sick, or sitting down for a cup of coffee to serve as a listening ear with a neighbor who is going through a difficult time in life.

MASKS OF GOD

Perhaps the most significant contribution by Luther in his theological understanding of vocation is the mystery that all stations and offices in the horizontal plane of life, be they exercised by a believer or an unbeliever, in actuality serve as masks for God. Luther expounds on this mystery of the

---

180. Luther, "Sermon on the Mount," 448.

Luther's Teaching on Vocation

hiddenness of God behind man's work as a mask when he explains, "Thus the Lord is at work in all things. Man must plow, reap, sow; but he is God's mask."[181] In his master's thesis on "The Masks of God," Rev. Dr. Anthony Steinbronn reflects on Luther's theological understanding of the *Larvae Dei* (mask of God). He explains that God wears masks in dealing with humanity, working in ways that cannot be seen, except through the eyes of faith.[182] Wingren notes the significance of this in Luther's teaching on vocation when he states, "God himself will milk the cows through him whose vocation that is."[183] As such God works in a hidden way through the means of each person's daily labor to bring his care and blessing to the world, oftentimes in spite of humanity's sinfulness.

While God works through the vocation of believers in their daily stations of life without their knowledge, with increased awareness of this mystery can come greater cooperation with God's purposes in the world. Luther discusses this when he teaches on Ps 147:

> What else is all our work to God—whether in the fields, in the garden, in the city, in the house, in war, or in government—but just such a child's performance, by which He wants to give His gifts in the fields, at home, and everywhere else? These are the masks of God, behind which He wants to remain concealed and do all things.... God gives all good gifts; but you must lend a hand and take the bull by the horns; that is, you must work and thus give God good cause and a mask.[184]

When, through faith, we submit to God's purpose in our vocation, we become greater conduits of God's love in service to our neighbor. There is increased intentionality in our daily interactions with those around us. Our eyes become open to our neighbor's needs. Our hearts are more inclined to find ways to be a blessing as we seek to serve them. As Wingren states so well, "He who by faith is open to God is by love open to his neighbor."[185] Through that faith of believers, God moves in love toward his creation by means of vocation.

---

181. Wingren, *Luther on Vocation*, 138.
182. Steinbronn, "Masks of God," 1.
183. Wingren, *Luther on Vocation*, 9.
184. Luther, "Selected Psalms III," 115.
185. Wingren, *Luther on Vocation*, 161.

COMMON GRACE AND SAVING GRACE

As God works in a hidden way through the vocation of believers, there are two end goals he has in mind. The first is that we serve as conduits of his common grace, which is his care and provision for the world.[186] Creation was not a one-time event. It is, as Kolden says, the ongoing creative act of God in which he is "continually creating and preserving or we and everything would cease to be."[187] In his explanation of the fourth petition of the Lord's Prayer, where we are instructed by Jesus to pray for our daily bread, Luther describes this care and preservation for the world in this way:

> *What is meant by daily bread?* Daily bread includes everything that has to do with the support and needs of the body, such as food and drink, clothing, shoes, house, home, land, animals, money, goods, a devout husband or wife, devout children, devout workers, devout and faithful rulers, good government, good weather, peace, health, self-control, good reputation, good friends, faithful neighbors, and the like.[188]

Some of these blessings of daily bread such as "good weather," come to us as God works in a hidden way through creation itself. However, many of these gifts of common grace that Luther describe come to us from God working through the means of people fulfilling their areas of responsibility in life. In a very real way, vocation is not just about our call to love and serve our neighbor in the everyday duties of our lives. It is also about God loving and serving our neighbor through us.

For believers specifically, there is also a second end goal that God has in mind for our vocation. It is not only that we serve as conduits for his common grace to the world, but that we would also become conduits of his saving grace as well. In, perhaps, one of the most remarkable statements by Luther in his collection of writings, he describes how we are called to this task as we live as Christ to our neighbors:

> Hence, as our heavenly Father has in Christ freely come to our aid, we also ought freely to help our neighbor through our body and its works, and each one should become as it were a Christ to the other

---

186. Benne, *Ordinary Saints*, 77–78.
187. Kolden, *Christian's Calling*, 18.
188. Luther, *Luther's Small Catechism*, 18–19.

that we may be Christs to one another and Christ may be the same in all, that is, that we may be truly Christians.[189]

Through the means of grace, we not only grow in our faith in Christ, but Jesus becomes our identity. And as we receive Christ through the Word and Sacraments, Luther says that Christ now dwells in us.[190]

As a result, we are now called to be as Christ to our neighbor as Jesus neighbors us. This neighboring is not only about loving and serving our neighbors with our deeds, but also about sharing the saving love of Jesus with them as well. In the book *Who Am I?* Chad Lakies explains that part of a believer's vocation in Christ is to serve as priests like Christ, being called to call others to faith in Jesus. To this point he states, "God also uses us to tell the story, to call others to believe. You might say, then, that one of our callings, as Christians, is to call others to hear and believe the gospel of Jesus, who gave his life for us that we might live fully in him."[191] The daily responsibilities of believers in their callings in life provide ample opportunities to be the means of both God's common as well as his saving grace.

DISCERNING GOD'S WILL IN VOCATION

With this overview of Luther's theological understanding of vocation established, the question now becomes, how does a believer begin to discern and live out their callings in life in practical terms? Broadly speaking, Luther's teaching on vocation provides a comprehensive framework for understanding God's will and purposes for believers in all aspects of their lives. A believer has been called by faith in their vertical relationship with Christ, through their baptism, to be a child of God and a member of the Priesthood of All Believers. They have also been called in their horizontal relationships to love and serve their neighbors in all of their areas of responsibilities in life. Luther sums this teaching up, and the freedom this gives believers in terms of seeking God's will for their lives, when he writes, "For only two things are necessary: faith and love. Everything else you are free to do or to leave undone."[192] All else is free when it comes to faith before God, for Jesus paid it all, and the guiding variable for action is love when it comes to

---

189. Luther, "Freedom of a Christian," 620.
190. Lull, *Luther's Basic Theological Writings*, 620.
191. Lakies, "Identity," 9.
192. Wingren, *Luther on Vocation*, 95.

one's neighbor, depending on their need.[193] Ultimately, when it comes to a believer living out their vocation, as Wingren states, "It is only in faith and the Spirit that God's will is effected."[194]

As a result, believers have incredible freedom when it comes to living a life aligned to God's will, as long as they have faith in God and love for one's neighbor. Luther highlights this freedom when he states, "By way of comparison one might say that the gospel has left us in the hand of our own counsel, to have dominion over things and use them as we wish; but Moses and the pope have not left us to that counsel, but have coerced us with laws and have subjected us rather to their own choice."[195] Part of understanding God's will for life does come from the role a believer is fulfilling at any given moment in their vocations.[196] However, Christian love for one's neighbor, prompted by faith, rises above all laws, for love is the fulfillment of the believer's vocation.[197] Wingren emphasizes this point when he states, "There is freedom to do, if love to another requires it, and freedom not to do, if that is what love to one's neighbor requires. Through such freedom of action faith and relationship to God have real significance for the shaping of vocation. Life according to vocation never becomes fixed or rigid."[198] As such, believers cannot rely on old patterns to follow, which apply in all situations, making imitating others unnecessary and inadequate.[199] Love acts as it pleases as it discerns God's will toward one's neighbor.[200]

The freedom a believer has in terms of living out their calling in Christ in their various areas of responsibilities in life opens up possibilities when it comes to discerning God's will. A person need not leave one's vocation to follow God's will, nor is it wrong to do so. Mark Paustian, in an article entitled "Unleashing Our Calling" given at a symposium on vocation at Wisconsin Lutheran Seminary in 2006, describes that after a time of discernment and prayer, "One is free to follow 'a more burning Yes,' and to pursue a new vocation."[201] After having reflected how thankful he was that

---

193. Wingren, *Luther on Vocation*, 49.
194. Wingren, *Luther on Vocation*, 970–71.
195. Luther, "Bondage of the Will," 119.
196. Kolden, *Christian's Calling*, 33.
197. Wingren, *Luther on Vocation*, 120.
198. Wingren, *Luther on Vocation*, 96.
199. Wingren, *Luther on Vocation*, 233.
200. Wingren, *Luther on Vocation*, 99.
201. Paustian, "Unleashing Our Calling," 13.

Luther left the monastery, Paustian explained the freedom believers have in discerning God's will in terms of their vocations in life when he stated:

> A thousand opportunities confront the believer, all of which conform to God's law. There need be no ringing of hands, God's mercy being what it is, when the choice is "between good and good." You choose one option knowing it would not have been a sin to choose another. It is like entering a department store, ambling up to a certain shelf in a certain department until your eyes fall on the item that seizes your gaze, the one you select just for your Father. You will crawl up into his lap. He will peel off the wrapping and exclaim, "Oh and what a delight!" This is grace.[202]

Instead of closing down options, Luther's teaching on vocation opens up possibilities for believers when it comes to seeking to live a life aligned to God's will. It may encourage believers as they persevere in their current areas of responsibilities, or it may open up new directions and new opportunities in life in terms of their vocation.[203] It also counters the notion that God's will for a believer's life is limited to one choice. There are many options available to a believer, from what career to pursue, whom to marry, where to live, etc., that all fall within God's will. All the while, believers can trust that as they plan today, they have confidence that God is at work in and through their lives, calling them to his purposes according to his will.[204]

However, while the Christian is free in determining how they will carry out their calling in love and service to their neighbor in any given situation, this does not mean that vocation is entirely self-determined for believers. God's will and providence ultimately prevails in the life of a believer in terms of their vocation. In Prov 19:21 (NIV) we hear, "Many are the plans in a person's heart, but it is the LORD's purpose that prevails." It is Veith who highlights how it is God who is, ultimately, the one who calls believers into their vocations in life when he writes,

> One aspect of the doctrine of vocation flies in the face of every self-help book and occupational seminar, every conversation about "your plans," and every agonizing bout of decision-making. Despite what our culture leads us to believe, vocation is not

---

202. Paustian, "Unleashing Our Calling," 13–14.
203. Kolden, *Christian's Calling*, 30.
204. Veith, *God at Work*, 54.

self-chosen. That is to say, we do not choose our vocations. We are called to them.[205]

Our callings in the horizontal plane of life come from outside of ourselves, mediated by God working through other people utilizing their vocations in life.[206] Veith notes that one does not choose what family or country they are born into or how they may decide to get married, but someone else must say yes.[207] Believers are also given unique talents and gifts, specifically by God, that can lead them to certain career choices and influences the ways a believer will love and serve their neighbor.[208] Lakies affirms this idea of one's callings coming from beyond themselves when he writes, "That a vocation is a calling signals the fact that there's someone doing the calling—there's another agent in the mix, someone calling you and drawing you toward a particular kind of life."[209] One may work, plan, and prepare; however, it is ultimately God's will that confirms a believer's vocations in life.[210]

Another aspect of discerning God's will in living out one's vocation in life is that, strictly speaking, a believer's calling is not so much a future destination to be discovered but is given presently in life.[211] While one may rightly prepare for some future goal, a believer should not lose sight of the reality that God has given them holy callings in their daily areas of responsibilities today.[212] As Veith notes, "Perhaps later, another vocation will present itself. But vocation is to be found not simply in future career decisions, but in the here and now."[213] Veith's statement echoes Luther's teaching on the present reality of one's callings when he states,

> Therefore do not follow your own counsels and desires, but do what your hand finds before it. That is, continue in the definite work given you and commanded by God, eschewing such things as would hinder you. Thus Samuel said to Saul, "You will be changed into a different man, and what your hand finds to do, do it, etc." He did not prescribe a law to him, but whatever presented itself must

---

205. Veith, *God at Work*, 50.
206. Veith, *God at Work*, 54–55.
207. Veith, *God at Work*, 50.
208. Veith, *Spirituality of the Cross*, 80.
209. Lakies, "Identity," 6–7.
210. Veith, *God at Work*, 57.
211. Veith, *God at Work*, 57.
212. Veith, *God at Work*, 58.
213. Veith, *Spirituality of the Cross*, 80.

be accepted, and there is the work to be done. And so Solomon speaks here: Always pursue that which is present to your hands and belongs to your vocation. If you are a preacher or a minister of the Word of God, continue in the reading of the Scripture and in the office of teaching, not wishing to be carried into something else till the Lord takes you. For whatever the Lord has not said or commanded will be of no advantage.[214]

Ultimately, a believer's vocation is to love and serve the neighbors God has placed before them today in their family, church, workplace, and community. Veith notes that finding one's vocation is primarily about discovering the part we play in God's grand design of loving and serving our neighbors.[215] To act outside of the calling God has placed before a believer in their various areas of responsibility in life would only create trouble, frustration, and wasted time.[216]

So, how does a believer practically discern God's will for their life in terms of their daily callings? It is Benne who explains that while sometimes an individual may be able to discern God's will in terms of their calling individually, usually vocational discernment comes through conversations with fellow believers.[217] The value of these interactions aids a believer in the discernment process, as well as provides accountability for decisions made.[218] In terms of identifying God's will for a believer in regards to their vocations in life, it is not only a matter of praying for open doors but also may involve opening doors. Benne describes this when he states, "We must decide, most often with colleagues, what doors need to be opened. Then we plan, strategize, and act in concert to achieve the goals we aim at. In other words, instead of doors opening, one aims at opening doors."[219] This process involves being open to possibilities and rethinking strategies.[220] Benne also notes, discerning God's will involves being committed for a long time when a path is decided upon (disciplined attachment) and knowing when to move on when a role is no longer a good fit (disciplined detachment).[221]

---

214. Wingren, *Luther on Vocation*, 226–27.
215. Veith, *God at Work*, 60.
216. Veith, *God at Work*, 139.
217. Benne, *Ordinary Saints*, 106.
218. Benne, *Ordinary Saints*, 106.
219. Benne, *Ordinary Saints*, 106.
220. Benne, *Ordinary Saints*, 106.
221. Benne, *Ordinary Saints*, 106.

Who Have You Been Called to Be?

Finally, in regards to an author that Benne references, Frederick Buechner, in his book *Wishful Thinking*, offers some helpful advice for discovering and living out one's vocations in life, "The place God calls you to is the place where your deep gladness and the world's deep hunger meet."[222] At this intersection of one's God-given gifts and talents, and the need of one's neighbors, calling and God's will can often be discerned.

In closing, it is Benne who provides practical guidance for vocational discernment by assisting believers in creating awareness around God's will for their lives:

1. Believers must first gain clarity about themselves as they realistically assess their own talents, gifts, capacities, and passions in life.
2. Second, believers must gain awareness about the needs of their world and specifically their specific neighbors that they have been called to love and serve in their various areas of responsibility in life.
3. Third, led by the guidance of the Holy Spirit, believers seek to discern their unique calling at the intersection of their talents and gifts and the needs of their world.
4. Fourth, believers step into God's will for their life by taking on the responsibilities given in their various callings in life through "disciplined attachment."
5. Finally, believers may also need to step away from certain responsibilities in order to take on any new responsibilities that God is calling them to through "disciplined detachment."[223]

---

222. Buechner, *Wishful Thinking*, 95.
223. Benne, *Ordinary Saints*, 104–7.

3

Vocational Coaching

FINDING MY PLACE IN THE WORLD

"What does this mean?" This is a question that many who are familiar with *Luther's Small Catechism* know very well. At the end of each catechetical teaching, as Luther presents the six chief parts of the Christian faith (the Ten Commandments, the Apostles' Creed, the Lord's Prayer, the Sacrament of Holy Baptism, Confession, and the Sacrament of the Altar), he follows up with the question "What does this mean?" For Luther, it was not enough for those learning the Christian faith to grasp faith's content. Throughout his many responses to this question, there are not only those things he taught that one should avoid as prohibitions but also positive encouragement of those things believers should do. Luther intended that those catechized in the Christian faith would practically live out their calling in Christ in all of their areas of responsibility in daily life.

"What does this mean?" This is a question that many believers who learn about Luther's teaching on vocation might find themselves asking. It is one thing to intellectually grasp the content of Luther's theological framework on vocation. Yet, it is another thing to personally understand how his teaching applies to one's daily life in practical, down-to-earth terms. It's like a person trying to figure out where a puzzle piece fits into a ten-thousand-piece jigsaw puzzle set. They may understand what the puzzle is supposed to look like when completed from the picture on the puzzle box. However, they may struggle to figure out where that one piece fits into the whole or where to begin placing it. Now consider how much more difficult it would be if they were blindfolded. They would struggle to see not only how all the pieces fit together, but they would also be blind to the nature and shape of the puzzle piece they were holding in their hand. Many believers have the same struggle as they consider where they fit into the grand scheme of God's working in our world today. It is one thing to get the big picture. It is another thing to begin to discern where one fits into what God is doing around them, especially if one doesn't even know the nature and shape of God's gifting and design in their own life.

In his book *You Lost Me*, David Kinnaman describes this struggle that many millennials who grew up in the church have in discerning how their calling in Christ connects to their callings in life.[1] As a result, many young people are dropping out of the church. Back in 2011, when Kinnaman wrote *You Lost Me*, 59 percent of young adults with a Christian background dropped out of church involvement. Now, according to his book *Faith for Exiles*, less than a decade later, that number is 64 percent.[2] Ultimately, he identifies the dropout problem as a disciple-making problem.[3] In addressing this dropout concern, Kinnaman identifies three significant gaps in the disciple-making process with young people. He addresses one of these gaps, the lack of discipleship focused around discovering and living out one's vocation, when he writes,

> The second arena is vocation, that powerful, often ignored intersection of faith and calling. Millions of Christ-following teens and young adults are interested in serving in mainstream professions, such as science, law, media, technology, education, law enforcement, military, the arts, business, marketing and advertising, healthcare, accounting, psychology, and dozens of others. Yet, most receive little guidance from their church communities for how to connect these vocational dreams with their faith in Christ.[4]

Vocation is more than what one does for a living, hence this reflection highlights the challenges many young believers experience as they leave home. They struggle in understanding how their faith in Jesus that they experience in their church relates to their various areas of responsibility in this post-church and post-Christian culture that they find themselves in today. Among many believers there is still a distinction that church is

---

1. Kinnaman, *You Lost Me*, 11.
2. Kinnaman and Matlock, *Faith for Exiles*, 14–15.
3. Kinnaman, *You Lost Me*, 21.
4. Kinnaman, *You Lost Me*, 29.

sacred while the world, and all it offers, is considered secular. As such, faith in Jesus can begin to appear irrelevant or disconnected to daily life. Like these young people, many believers are left asking the question "What does this mean?" as they struggle to figure out how their faith translates to the reality of their everyday lives.

The antidote that Kinnaman asserts to bridge this disconnect between faith in Christ and one's vocations in life comes down to the process of discipleship. The problem, he argues, is that we have tended towards discipleship in a mass production, one-size-fits-all approach.[5] Kinnaman explains his contention when he writes, "But disciples cannot be mass-produced. Disciples are handmade, one relationship at a time."[6] According to Kinnaman, "We need new ecosystems of spiritual and vocational apprenticeship that can support deeper relationships and more vibrant faith formation.... We need to renew our catechisms and confirmations—not because we need new theology, but because their current forms too rarely produce young people of deep, abiding faith."[7] In his view, what is needed today is a new, personalized approach to discipleship that prepares believers, young and old, not only to grow in their faith in Jesus but also to live that faith out practically in the world they experience on a daily basis beyond the walls of their church.

Coaching can provide just such a means to personally disciple believers today to connect their vertical calling in Christ to their horizontal callings of life. Additionally, coaching can help believers discover and live out God's workmanship and design in love and service to their neighbors. Through this kind of vocational coaching, the church can empower this generation to connect the puzzle pieces of how they can uniquely live out their faith in everyday life, moving beyond the secular/sacred divide to living a holistic faith. In the book *20 and Something*, David H. Kim speaks of the need for this kind of vocational discipleship:

> Here of course, the church has something to give. But first it is going to have to learn how to genuinely connect the dots—from vocation to prayer life to Instagram feed—for a life of meaning. Our research shows just how important this holistic integration of faith is. Among churchgoing millennials, 45 percent have learned to understand their gifts and passions as part of God's calling,

---

5. Kinnaman, *You Lost Me*, 13.
6. Kinnaman, *You Lost Me*, 13.
7. Kinnaman, *You Lost Me*, 13.

while 83 percent of church dropouts say the church has not helped them to learn this.[8]

Coaching is not discipleship per se. However, it is an ideal process which I personally have utilized to empower believers to discern and live out their unique calling in life for kingdom impact in a personalized and relevant way. It also provides a way for the church to nurture the giftedness of believers—their God-given calling, passions, and gifts—in love and service to others in their areas of responsibilities in life. With 75 percent of adults looking for ways to live a more meaningful life, vocational coaching can help believers and unbelievers alike, begin to answer that uniquely Lutheran question "What does this mean?"[9]

WHAT IS COACHING?

When it comes to the concept of coaching, there are also many who are asking the question "What does this mean?" The Merriam-Webster Dictionary explains that the origins of the word "coach" comes from the word *kocsi*, literally referring to wagons first made and produced in Kocs, Hungary. This was "a large usually closed four-wheeled horse-drawn carriage having doors in the sides and an elevated seat in front for the driver."[10] A coach was used to transport a person from one location to another. While the driver knew the possible routes to take, it was the passenger who determined the destination. A modern-day understanding of the concept of a coach may be that of a limo, taxi, or Uber service. With a press of a button on an app, a driver arrives to help transport you from one location to another of your choosing. Additionally, the word "coach" can refer to one who is a private tutor. This understanding connotes a personal supportive relationship focused on drawing knowledge out of a student, as opposed to a larger classroom setting of a teacher pouring knowledge in by instructing students. The word "coach" also can refer to one who instructs and trains, specifically in the realm of sports. All of these are correct starting points for understanding what coaching is as we consider its development over the last few decades in the workplace and beyond.

---

8. Kim, *20 and Something*, 28.
9. Barna Group, *Christians at Work*, 17.
10. Merriam-Webster, "Coach."

Vocational Coaching

In their book *Coaching for Christian Leaders* Linda Miller and Chad Hall explain how coaching is similar to the idea of the original meaning of the word in regards to a four-wheeled wagon when they write, "Today, coaching is similar. Coaching is still about forward movement and action. A Coach, however, is no longer a physical vehicle like a car. A coach is a person who facilitates actions that transport people from one place to another, from where they are to a new destination."[11] Analogous to the horse-drawn carriages of old, those who seek coaching for their personal life or in the context of business still set the destination of what it is that they would like to focus on as far as their "destination," while the coach is the one who knows the path to help the PBC (person being coached) get there. In this sense, coaching is moving people from where they are to where they want to be.

The concept of coaching seen in the world of sports is also one that many people are familiar with today. However, instead of seeing life and executive coaching in terms of a football coach who functions as the expert telling a group of players what to do in the game, it might be better to view coaching through the lens of a tennis coach, which is more of a personal one-on-one relationship. A significant influence on the development of coaching in the sports world and beyond was Timothy Gallwey when he wrote his book *The Inner Game of Tennis*, first published in 1974. He contended that the work of a coach was not just about mastery of skills but assisting those he coached to remove inner obstacles like nervousness, self-doubt, and self-condemnation to improve their performance.[12] Soon afterwards, John Whitmore partnered with Timothy Gallwey to apply his coaching principles to the world of business.[13] In his book, *Coaching for Performance*, Whitmore discusses the application of Gallwey's contribution to coaching when he states, "And Gallwey had put his finger on the essence of coaching. Coaching is unlocking people's potential to maximize their own performance. It is helping people to learn rather than teaching them."[14] Thus, the field of coaching beyond the world of sports was born.

Tapping into this imagery of coaching from the sporting world in the development and philosophy of life and executive coaching, Frederic Hudson, in his book *The Handbook of Coaching*, writes,

---

11. Miller and Hall, *Coaching for Christian Leaders*, 9.
12. Gallwey, *Inner Game of Tennis*, 2.
13. Whitmore, *Coaching for Performance*, 12.
14. Whitmore, *Coaching for Performance*, 10.

> Used in the athletic sense, coach is now widely applied to a person who facilitates experiential learning that results in future-oriented abilities. The term, as I use it, refers to a person who is a trusted role model, adviser, wise person, friend, mensch, steward, or guide—a person who works with emerging human and organizational forces to tap new energy and purpose, to shape new visions and plans, and to generate desired results. A coach is someone trained and devoted to guiding others to increased competence, commitment, and confidence.[15]

Hudson's description begins to define the field of coaching outside of sports as applied in the contexts of life and business. In his view, coaching is a supportive relationship that is focused on helping others gain the competence, commitment, and confidence they need within to achieve their visions and goals in life. Whitmore describes the outcomes of this type of coaching relationship between a coach and the PBC when he explains, "Self-belief, self-motivation, choice, clarity, commitment, awareness, responsibility, and action are the products of coaching."[16]

There are many excellent definitions of coaching out there that can help one begin to understand what coaching is and its potential benefits. However, a few examples would be valuable to gain a clearer picture of what coaching is and what coaching is not. One definition that is especially valuable for obtaining clarity on coaching comes from Gary Collins, in his book *Christian Coaching*, as he describes coaching in the following way:

> At its core, coaching equips people to move from where they are toward the greater competence and fulfillment they desire. Stated concisely, coaching is the art and practice of enabling individuals and groups to move from where they are to where they want to be. Coaching helps people expand their visions, build their confidence, unlock their potential, increase their skills, and take practical steps toward their goals.[17]

Collins's description of coaching is about assisting others as a coach to understand where they currently are in life, envision where they want to be in the future, explore ways to get there, and overcome obstacles that might get in the way.[18] His definition also helps one understand that coaching,

---

15. Hudson, *Handbook of Coaching*, 6.
16. Whitmore, *Coaching for Performance*, 39.
17. Collins, *Christian Coaching*, 14.
18. Collins, *Christian Coaching*, 100.

while typically best understood as a one-on-one relationship, can also be used in working with groups and teams to achieve collective goals. Many of Gallwey's contributions to coaching are reflected in this definition.

Another helpful definition of coaching comes from Jeffrey Auerbach, who heads up the College of Executive Coaching, my original coach training program that I went through shortly after discovering coaching. In his book *Personal and Executive Coaching* Auerbach explains coaching as:

> Personal coaching involves helping generally well-functioning people create and achieve goals, maximize personal development, and navigate transitions on the path to realizing their ideal vision for the current and emerging chapters of their lives. Most personal coaching clients are focused on the development of an ideal future self, an ideal career, or an improved family life. The coach aids the client through the coaching conversation in developing a coaching agenda, incorporating values clarification, identification of strengths, and articulation of the client's current life and career purpose. The coach supports the client's efforts to engage in life-long learning, navigate any obstacles, delegate or let go of energy-draining situations, honors challenges, and celebrates successes.[19]

For those struggling with hurts and pains from the past, those issues are ideally suited for counseling rather than coaching, which will be addressed later on in this section on the distinction between coaching and other helping professions. Coaching works best with those who are generally considered healthy and well-adjusted in life who want to envision and work towards a preferred future. It makes the assumption that people are capable of assuming responsibility for working towards the results they desire in life. In their book *Co-Active Coaching* Henry and Karen Kimsey-House assert this basic assumption of those that seek coaching, "They are capable: capable of finding answers; capable of choosing; capable of taking action; capable of recovering when things don't go as planned; and, especially, capable of learning. This capacity is wired into all human beings no matter their circumstances."[20] As such, coaching seeks to empower others to be self-sufficient in life, not make them dependent on the coach.

Perhaps the most concise definition of coaching comes from the International Coaching Federation (ICF), which is currently the largest professional coaching organization in the world. They define coaching in

---

19. Auerbach, *Personal and Executive Coaching*, 10.
20. Kimsey-House et al., *Co-Active Coaching*, 3.

the following way, "ICF defines coaching as partnering with clients in a thought-provoking and creative process that inspires them to maximize their personal and professional potential."[21] Coaching is truly a partnership between the coach and the PBC. Working in collaboration around the client's agenda, the coach empowers the PBC to develop, grow, and achieve their goals.[22] In their book *Adaptive Coaching* Terry Bacon and Laurie Voss describe that the coach does not provide the content of the coaching conversation—that comes from the client. Keith Webb, in his book *The COACH Model*, explains that what the coach instead brings is a process that draws the content out of the coachee.[23] As such, coaching is client-directed, where the PBC, not the coach, sets the agenda for the focus of the coaching engagement.[24] Ultimately, as Collins notes, "Coaching is a form of servant leadership that involves encouraging or challenging people to pursue their goals and fulfill their potential."[25] Jane Creswell, in her book *Coaching for Excellence*, reflects on how coaching is especially good for tapping into an individual's untapped potential.[26]

It is important to note that there are some different approaches to coaching. Bacon and Voss explain how coaching can either be "circumstantial" or "programmatic." Circumstantial coaching is typically more spontaneous and short-term in duration.[27] This type of coaching often arises from the circumstances of the day, and the PBC typically knows what they want from coaching, usually focused on changing or improving their performance.[28] There is also programmatic coaching, which is a long-term commitment (months to a year), in which the coach actively invests in the coachee's growth and development.[29] This programmatic coaching approach is more typical of a formalized coaching process that involves a coaching agreement.[30]

---

21. ICF, "About ICF."
22. Bacon and Voss, *Adaptive Coaching*, 182.
23. Webb, *COACH Model*, 33.
24. Miller and Hall, *Coaching for Christian Leaders*, 70.
25. Collins, *Christian Coaching*, 41.
26. Creswell, *Coaching for Excellence*, 12.
27. Bacon and Voss, *Adaptive Coaching*, 98.
28. Bacon and Voss, *Adaptive Coaching*, 98–99.
29. Bacon and Voss, *Adaptive Coaching*, 98–99.
30. Auerbach, *Personal and Executive Coaching*, 240.

Another distinction in coaching is what Chad Hall, with Coach Approach Ministries, calls "free-range" vs. "framework coaching."[31] Free-range coaching is where the coachee defines the agenda for a coaching engagement and the focus of each coaching session. In this way, coaching is client-directed. This approach to coaching is very much in line with what has been addressed previously. In framework coaching, the coach defines the focus of the coaching engagement and, typically, the coaching sessions as well, while the client is empowered to determine the actions they will take in response to this focus. Bacon and Voss address framework coaching when they state, "Development models help to establish a framework that makes sense to the client but also allows the coaching to unfold and the emphasis to change."[32] Some examples of framework coaching might be strengths coaching utilizing the CliftonStrengths®[33] assessment, coaching to increase the PBC's emotional intelligence, coaching to increase an individual's leadership capacity, improving one's time management, living a healthy lifestyle, etc.

Coaches as Creative Thinking Partners

A helpful metaphor in thinking about who a coach is and what they do is to think of them in terms of a creative think-partner. Auerbach reflects on this metaphor when he states, "Coaches serve as collaborative thinking partners and encourage the exploration of their clients' rationales, a process that can uncover errors, biases, and opportunities."[34] There are often things that people are thinking about, yet they don't have anyone to "think out loud" with in their lives in a creative and constructive way. Coaching moves this thinking from an internal monological conversation to an external dialogical conversation. It makes the thinking visible to both the coach and, most importantly, to the PBC. According to Robert Hargrove in his book *Masterful Coaching*, "Being a thinking partner often starts with simplifying people's thought processes but without overlooking complexity."[35] As such, in a non-

---

31. Miller, "Framework Coaching."

32. Bacon and Voss, *Adaptive Coaching*, 100.

33. Gallup®, CliftonStrengths® and the CliftonStrengths 34 Themes of Talent are trademarks of Gallup, Inc. All rights reserved.

34. Auerbach, *Personal and Executive Coaching*, 17.

35. Hargrove, *Masterful Coaching*, 54.

judgmental manner, the coach serves the coachee as a sounding board to help them explore ideas and come up with their own discoveries.[36]

History and Development of Coaching

According to Hudson, the field of life and executive coaching began developing in the 1980s.[37] These early pioneers of coaching in the business field helped develop visioning processes, leadership training, executive coaching, and transition management.[38] In their book *Faith Coaching*, Chad Hall, Bill Copper, and Kathryn McElveen explain this development in this new field of coaching when they write,

> People who were into personal development and came from psychology, counseling and consulting backgrounds began to hone their professional skills according to a radical (yet timeless) philosophy: what if people already knew most of the answers to their questions and already had the potential to reach many of their dreams.[39]

A significant rationale behind the development and growth of this new field of coaching was the need for visioning and strategic planning, given many of the adaptive challenges leaders and organizations experienced in the face of the accelerating speed of change in the late twentieth century.[40] In 1995, the ICF was formed to help develop high standards for coaching, coach certification, and a global network of accredited coaches.[41]

Coaching is truly a multidisciplinary field, drawing from many conceptional and professional roots.[42] Hudson notes that there are two major fields that have influenced the development of coaching, "psychological theories of adult development, including psychosocial stage theories, and social theories of adult development."[43] In Hudson's view, the psychotherapy theory that informs coaching the most is solution-focused therapy. As he notes in regard

---

36. Hargrove, *Masterful Coaching*, 55.
37. Hudson, *Handbook of Coaching*, 4.
38. Hudson, *Handbook of Coaching*, 4.
39. Hall et al., *Faith Coaching*, 19.
40. Hudson, *Handbook of Coaching*, 4.
41. Hall et al., *Faith Coaching*, 19.
42. Hudson, *Handbook of Coaching*, 67.
43. Hudson, *Handbook of Coaching*, 67.

to this approach, "Instead of treating pathology, the therapist develops the competence of the client. In this modality the therapist becomes a personal consultant, pursuing with the client what the client would be like beyond whatever the presenting clinical problem might be."[44] With this influence, coaching seeks to not dwell on past hurts and issues, but, instead, on future-focused solutions to the opportunities and challenges of life.

In explaining the history and development of coaching, Auerbach additionally describes this multidisciplinary nature and development of coaching when he writes,

> Much of the recent research on coaching theory and practice has been based on applying psychological theories to the practice of coaching, including Carl Rogers's person-centered approach, cognitive psychology, behavioral psychology, developmental psychology and adult learning theory, family therapy, social psychology, emotional intelligence, positive psychology, and even psychotherapy.[45]

While he notes that the process and skills of coaching are similar to therapy, they are very distinct in significant ways.[46] In his view, psychotherapy, for example, usually focuses on alleviating illnesses and trauma within a person, whereas coaching focuses on achievement and fulfillment in generally well-functioning individuals.[47] Another influence that can be seen in coaching is Maslow's hierarchy of needs as a coach helps the PBC work towards a life of self-actualization.[48]

A recent school of thought that has had a significant impact on coaching in recent times is the developing field of positive psychology. Robert Biswas-Diener and Ben Dean, in their book *Positive Psychology Coaching*, reflect on the distinctive nature of positive psychology verses the primary emphasis of psychology in the past when they explain that instead of focusing on what is wrong with people and how to fix it, positive psychology focuses on what is right with people and builds on it.[49] In his book *Flourish* Martin Seligman, known as the father of positive psychology, explains that, at its core, positive psychology focuses on improving well-being and

---

44. Hudson, *Handbook of Coaching*, 75.
45. Bacon and Voss, *Adaptive Coaching*, xxii.
46. Auerbach, *Personal and Executive Coaching*, 6.
47. Auerbach, *Personal and Executive Coaching*, 6.
48. Auerbach, *Personal and Executive Coaching*, 24.
49. Biswas-Diener and Dean, *Positive Psychology Coaching*, 11.

building a life that is worth living.[50] Seligman lays out the case for how his scientific, evidence-based approach to discovering what leads to people thriving and flourishing in life can serve as a theoretical backbone to the field of coaching.[51] He advocates that coaching can be especially effective in working with people around the five areas of life where individuals find fulfillment: positive emotions, engagement, good relationships, meaning, and accomplishments (PERMA model).[52] In Seligman's view, "Coaching with these evidence-based interventions and validated measures of well-being will set the boundaries of a responsible coaching practice."[53]

Coaching vs. Other Helping Professions

Since coaching is a relatively new field that is still developing, there can be some confusion about what coaching is and what coaching is not. Part of this misunderstanding comes from confusing coaching with other helping professions. Miller and Hall note the distinction of coaching from other service professionals when they explain, "Professional coaching is a distinct service that focuses on an individual's life as it relates to goal setting, outcome creation, and personal change management."[54] It is not to say that these other helping professions are not valuable and appropriate in their proper settings. However, coaching is the preferred approach in specific contexts. Miller and Hall list some of these settings where coaching is a good fit in working with others: "(1) a person is ready for the next level of development personally or professionally, (2) specific goals or tasks need to be accomplished, (3) a person demonstrates a desire to respond to change positively, (4) development is as important, or more important, than the task or goal, (5) there's a sense of a new season of life and it's time to prepare."[55] All of these are good indications that a person will benefit from coaching.

With this distinction in mind regarding what coaching is, the first helping profession to contrast it with is counseling and therapy. As was addressed before, coaching is generally distinct from counseling and therapy

50. Seligman, *Flourish*, 1–2.
51. Seligman, *Flourish*, 70.
52. Seligman, *Flourish*, 70–71.
53. Seligman, *Flourish*, 71.
54. Miller and Hall, *Coaching for Christian Leaders*, 125.
55. Miller and Hall, *Coaching for Christian Leaders*, 19.

regarding its focus and aim. In *Christ-Centered Coaching*, Jane Creswell notes this distinction when she explains, "Counseling is about resolving how the past informs the present, while coaching is only about the present and moving forward. Counseling assumes a lack of health, while coaching assumes health."[56] Coaching is distinctively future-focused and aims to promote growth and achieving goals within those who are, for the most part, healthy and well-adjusted individuals. Conversely, counseling tends to be past-focused and aims to heal pain, dysfunction, and conflict within people or between individuals.[57] A helpful analogy that serves well to make this distinction is to think about a person taking a trip. A coach is like one who helps a person determine a destination of where they want to go and helps them figure out how best to get there. However, if that person has too much baggage, the trip may be costly, or they won't be able to go at all. A counselor is like one who helps a person off-load some baggage so that they are free to take a trip to the destination they desire.

Another important distinction to make regarding helping professions is between coaching and mentoring. Often coaching gets confused with mentoring. A mentor tends to be someone who is an expert due to their field and experience and seeks to guide others in their development and growth.[58] Collins describes how coaching is distinct from mentoring when he writes,

> Whereas mentors may exemplify and share expert knowledge about vocational or spiritual issues, coaches do not claim to bring expertise or special knowledge about the client's area of interest. Coaches stand alongside of people who are coached, helping them envision their future directions, guiding as they avoid giving advice or specific suggestions.[59]

As such, mentors serve as experts who seek to shape those they mentor to be and do things like they do, whereas coaches recognize the PBC to be the expert of their own life and seek to empower them to be more of who they are in life. Bacon and Voss note that it is better for coaches not to have expertise in the subject matter being discussed with the PBC so that they are not tempted to give advice.[60] As Henry and Karen Kimsey-House note, "Ultimately, coaching is not about what the coach delivers but about

---

56. Creswell, *Christ-Centered Coaching*, 15.
57. Miller and Hall, *Coaching for Christian Leaders*, 125.
58. Miller and Hall, *Coaching for Christian Leaders*, 126.
59. Collins, *Christian Coaching*, 19.
60. Bacon and Voss, *Adaptive Coaching*, 23.

what clients create."[61] The goal of coaching is not for coaches to make little clones of themselves out of their clients.[62]

A third helping profession that sometimes gets confused with coaching is consulting. Consultants are those who engage with individuals and organizations because of their expertise, with their goal being to diagnose problems and offer solutions.[63] Collins makes the distinction of a coach from a consultant when he explains, "The consultant is an expert who analyzes and makes recommendations.... In contrast, coaching is much more focused on the individual or group being coached, stimulating these people to make their own judgments and decisions."[64] A coach is not a "man with a plan."[65] In their book *Coaching 101* Robert Logan and Sherilyn Carlton explain the uniqueness that coaching offers when they write, "Coaches don't need to know all the answers—they just need to know how to help people find them."[66] As such, coaches are experts in a process that leads others in self-discovery, not experts of what someone else should do. Mentors offer solutions that may or may not work for a context, whereas coaches help people, groups, and organizations develop solutions for themselves that are created for their context. This coaching approach empowers others to take ownership of the solutions upon which they decide. As a result, they are more likely to follow-through in what they decide to do rather than on actions proposed by a consultant.[67]

It is important to note that there is a strand of coaching called "directive coaching" that is similar to mentoring and consulting. Bacon and Voss acknowledge that in some circumstances directive coaching can be appropriate, especially in times when the coach's expertise is needed, when there is only one way to do something, or when there isn't enough time for nondirective coaching.[68] However, in their experience, they found more people prefer nondirective coaching over directive coaching. They note, "We think this is why 83 percent of clients we surveyed said they prefer coaches who ask questions rather than 'being told what to do.' Non-directive coaching

61. Kimsey-House et al., *Co-Active Coaching*, 20.
62. Creswell, *Christ-Centered Coaching*, 15.
63. Miller and Hall, *Coaching for Christian Leaders*, 125.
64. Collins, *Christian Coaching*, 17–18.
65. Creswell, *Christ-Centered Coaching*, 15.
66. Logan and Carlton, *Coaching 101*, 40.
67. Hall et al., *Faith Coaching*, 70.
68. Bacon and Voss, *Adaptive Coaching*, 93.

appeals to most people's need for self-sufficiency and self-directed growth."[69] Directive and nondirective coaching are not just two different approaches to coaching. They are radically different ways of seeing how people change and what motivates that change.[70] Directive coaching not only prevents people from learning how to solve problems independently, the advice the coach gives often proves to not work out in the end.[71] Regarding nondirective coaching, it is essential to note that while the coach intentionally guides the PBC through a process of self-discovery and analysis, they do so in a nonprescriptive way when it comes to the course of actions taken by the client. What the coachee does in response is for them to determine for themselves. Thus, this is what is meant by nondirective coaching.

The Shape and Flow of Coaching

As noted before, the coach is an expert in a process that they utilize in working with the PBC. While there are many coaching models available for coaches to use in working with a client, it is helpful to understand first the basic shape and flow of a typical coaching conversation. An excellent metaphor for understanding the structure of a coaching conversation is the hourglass model developed by Jane Creswell, found in her book *Coaching for Excellence*.[72]

---

69. Bacon and Voss, *Adaptive Coaching*, 96.
70. Bacon and Voss, *Adaptive Coaching*, 98.
71. Logan and Carlton, *Coaching 101*, 39.
72. Creswell, *Coaching for Excellence*, 6–7.

The Hourglass Model
Phases Of A Coach Approach

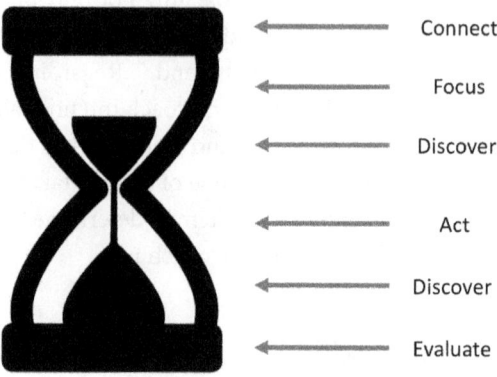

Figure 2. The Hourglass Model

The top of the hourglass represents where the coach "Connects" with the PBC for a coaching conversation. From there, a "Focus" for the coaching conversation is established. The conversation begins to narrow in focus as the coach works to help the client "Discover" all the perspectives and possibilities related to the topic. The narrow part of the hourglass represents the establishment of a specific focus that is actionable.[73] At this point, the coaching conversation begins to expand as the coach brainstorms options with the PBC, exploring all the possible ways to "Act" on this specific focus. Next, the coachee will "Discover" a strategy upon which they will act. Finally, the coach will "Evaluate" the PBC's commitment to this course of action, establish when they will act, and determine what encouragement and accountability they will need. Creswell explains that while not every coaching conversation will fit this hourglass model exactly, it is a helpful metaphor to keep in mind for how coaching flows.[74]

Coaching Models and "Dancing in the Moment"

As one considers the shape and flow of coaching, it is similar to dancing with a client in many ways. In this regard, there are several "dance steps" a

73. Miller and Hall, *Coaching for Christian Leaders*, 56.
74. Creswell, *Coaching for Excellence*, 7.

coach can use by way of coaching models to help guide the PBC through an intentional process leading to discovery and action. For example, Auerbach has developed the "CAACS" coaching model, which stands for "Connection" with the client, "Assessment" of their situation, "Articulation" of the desired focus, "Action" goals and steps, "Commitment" for what the PBC will do and when, and, finally, "Support" the coachee will need.[75] He also references the "5D Appreciative Coaching Model": "Define" the agenda, "Discover" information and resources, "Dream" of what could be, "Design" achievable steps to turn vision into reality, and "Deliver" the who, what, when, and how the changes will be implemented.[76] Another coaching model, developed by Whitmore, is known as the "GROW" model, which represents the following steps: "Goal" for the session, "Reality" of the situation, "Options" for strategy and action, and the "Will" to do it.[77] Collins has developed his own coaching approach, known as the "Basic Christian Coaching Model," with Jesus at the center of the wheel in his model. The coach helps the coachee assess each of the following steps in the coaching process with a Christ-centered focus: "Awareness" of where the client is now, "Vision" of where they want to go, "Strategy and Action" of how to get there, and "Obstacles" that get in the way.[78] These are but a few of the many different coaching models developed to help coaches move through the basic shape and flow of a coaching conversation with their clients, each with their distinctive process.

However, as a coach grows in their skill and experience, they learn to move and flow between these various coaching models—similar to how an expert dancer knows to blend many different dance styles given the particular music and circumstances. The ICF calls this skill "dancing in the moment" in relation to their coaching presence.[79] Collins explains this ability of a coach to dance in the moment with a client when he writes, "Dancing in the moment means the coach is able to discern through subtle surveillance the integration and needs of the person being coached and provide flexible response."[80] In any given moment, a masterful coach bends and flexes to the client's needs in the coaching conversation. As such, a

75. Auerbach, *Personal and Executive Coaching*, 32–39.
76. Auerbach, *Personal and Executive Coaching*, 105.
77. Whitmore, *Coaching for Performance*, 55.
78. Collins, *Christian Coaching*, 116–17.
79. ICF, "Minimum Skills Requirements."
80. Miller and Hall, *Coaching for Christian Leaders*, 51.

coach needs to be present in the moment and able to respond to what the PBC is saying rather than relying on some master plan going in beforehand or being restrained by any particular coaching model.[81]

Key Coaching Skills

While it is not the focus of this text to be a "how-to" book on coaching, it is important to discuss some of the critical skills coaches use in working with those they coach. Webb explains that coaches use a variety of coaching skills when he states, "Coaching involves listening to others, asking questions to deepen thinking, allowing others to find their own solutions, and doing it all in a way that makes people feel empowered and responsible enough to take action."[82] In particular, Collins observes that coaches use three especially essential skills in coaching: listening, asking powerful questions, and responding.[83] Miller and Hall assert that active listening and asking powerful questions are the two most essential coaching skills, making up 50 percent of a coaching conversation.[84] The purpose of these key coaching skills are geared to assist a person in understanding where they are, envisioning where they want to be, finding ways to get there, and overcoming any obstacles that stand in their way.[85] The following is an overview of some of the key coaching skills that coaches use in working with their coachees.

Active Listening

Like other helping professionals, such as counselors and therapists, coaches rely on active listening as an essential tool for the work they do with their clients. Highlighting this point, Logan and Carlton argue, "Listening is anything but passive. It is active and powerful, a significant tool that God has given us to use in the lives of others—for listening is the ultimate other-centered activity. A good listener focuses completely on the other person, giving that person undivided attention."[86] It is not just the content of what

81. Kimsey-House et al., *Co-Active Coaching*, 6.
82. Webb, *COACH Model*, 19–20.
83. Collins, *Christian Coaching*, 100.
84. Miller and Hall, *Coaching for Christian Leaders*, 22.
85. Collins, *Christian Coaching*, 100.
86. Logan and Carlton, *Coaching 101*, 34.

the PBC shares that a coach listens for as they work together. It is also the meaning behind what they say, the assumptions the coachee is making, and those things that are not said.[87] The coach is also listening for things like passion, themes, and insights that the client may not recognize. In essence, as Hall, Copper, and McElveen note, "A coach not only listens to the PBC, he also listens for her."[88] This listening does help a coach's understanding of the presented situation; however, it is more for the purpose of helping the PBC's understanding.

As a coach utilizes active listening in service to those they are coaching, they listen at three very distinct levels. Henry and Karen Kimsey-House discuss that there are three levels of listening. Level-one listening is what they coin "internal listening."[89] Listening at level one is listening by the coach to respond to what the PBC is saying. At this level the coach is more focused on their own thoughts as responses rather than genuinely listening to what the coachee is saying. Level-two listening is what they call "focused listening." This level of listening is where the coach focuses completely on hearing what the client is saying. And finally, they identify level-three listening as "global listening." This level of listening is where the coach is not just listening with their ears, but listening with their eyes. It is listening to not only focus on what is said but what is unsaid. Listening at level three is an intuitive level of listening. These three levels of listening serve as the gateway through which all coaching passes.[90] Active listening like this facilitates better questions for the coach and better discovery for the client.[91] For the coach, deep listening ultimately serves the client—it is to help facilitate learning for the PBC.[92]

Powerful Questions

In coaching, there is a cardinal rule that is widely accepted: "Ask, don't tell." About this rule in coaching, Logan and Carlton explain, "Never tell people something they can discover on their own."[93] The difference between a typi-

---

87. Miller and Hall, *Coaching for Christian Leaders*, 31.
88. Hall et al., *Faith Coaching*, 60.
89. Kimsey-House et al., *Co-Active Coaching*, 33–37.
90. Kimsey-House et al., *Co-Active Coaching*, 33–39.
91. Hall et al., *Faith Coaching*, 60.
92. Creswell, *Coaching for Excellence*, 44–45.
93. Logan and Carlton, *Coaching 101*, 53.

cal question and a powerful question is that the first extracts information while the second produces exploration within the PBC.[94] Curiosity is essential for coaches to have; however, it must always be in service to the coachee to promote discovery and problem-solving.[95] Creswell describes the impact that powerful questions can have when she writes, "A powerful question prompts discovery and generates new knowledge for the PBC, which now belongs to that person. Because the answer originated with the PBC, she will retain the information for much longer than if you simply told her the answer."[96] Powerful questions fuel the coaching conversation and empower the PBC to think and to act purposefully.[97]

What makes for a powerful question? First, powerful questions usually begin with "who, what, when, and how."[98] "Why" questions tend to be avoided because they can be too philosophical or sound judgmental. Most of the time a "why" question can be restated by a coach to probe motivation without falling into these pitfalls. Powerful questions are open-ended questions, which promote discovery for the PBC.[99] Closed-ended questions can lead to simple responses like yes or no. Whitmore explains why open-ended questions are preferred in coaching:

> Open questions requiring descriptive answers promote awareness, whereas closed questions are too absolute for accuracy, and yes or no answers close the door on the exploration of further detail.... Open questions are much more effective for generating awareness and responsibility in the coaching process.[100]

The goal of a coach is to open the door to discovery, not close it off. Also, powerful questions are best developed from the thought of what the PBC just said. Whitmore emphasizes this idea that the best questions build off of the last thing the coachee said when he states, "The principle is that questions should follow the interest and the train of thought of the coachee, not of the coach. If the coach leads the direction of the questions he will undermine that responsibility of the coachee."[101] In this way, the coach

---

94. Kimsey-House et al., *Co-Active Coaching*, 64.
95. Kimsey-House et al., *Co-Active Coaching*, 66.
96. Creswell, *Coaching for Excellence*, 46.
97. Miller and Hall, *Coaching for Christian Leaders*, 32.
98. Hall et al., *Faith Coaching*, 65.
99. Hall et al., *Faith Coaching*, 65.
100. Whitmore, *Coaching for Performance*, 46.
101. Whitmore, *Coaching for Performance*, 47–49.

is not directive with the PBC. They follow the client's train of thought, as Alice followed the white rabbit down the rabbit hole, helping the PBC make incredible discoveries in the process.

Direct Communication

While "ask, don't tell" is a cardinal rule for coaching, that doesn't mean that there isn't a role for direct communication with the coachee. According to Miller and Hall, "Delivering direct messages is one of the most powerful coaching skills. . . . Messages can be in the form of statements or questions. Either way, the purpose is to assist the person being coached in moving forward quickly and more deeply than normal conversations might."[102] Any direct communication that the coach uses should be short and concise, and is up to the PBC to accept or reject. It can be honest feedback based on witnessable observations designed to increase the coachee's awareness.[103] The key, if it is difficult feedback, is not to be judgmental.[104] Sometimes direct communication can come in the form of a word of encouragement.[105] Again, even words of encouragement are most effective when based on observations the coach has witnessed. Restating what the client just said in terms of a metaphor or analogy to help illustrate a point or paint a verbal picture can be a valuable gift for the coachee to increase their awareness.[106]

ICF Core-Competencies

These are but a few of the skills and competencies that an effective coach needs to develop and use in their coaching. All three of these skills (active listening, powerful questioning, and direct communication) were specifically addressed in the ICF's core-competencies prior to 2021.[107] Based on empirical data they collected, the ICF updated their core competencies in an effort to offer a simpler, more streamlined structure and integrate more

---

102. Miller and Hall, *Coaching for Christian Leaders*, 43.
103. Hargrove, *Masterful Coaching*, 102.
104. Auerbach, *Personal and Executive Coaching*, 117.
105. Collins, *Christian Coaching*, 111.
106. ICF, "ICF Core Competencies."
107. ICF, "ICF Core Competencies."

consistent, clear language.[108] The coaching skills of powerful questions and direct communication were folded into the new core-competency of "create awareness." The following are the new ICF core-competencies that went into effect in early 2021:

A. Foundation

1. Demonstrates Ethical Practice

Definition: Understands and consistently applies coaching ethics and standards of coaching.

2. Embodies a Coaching Mindset

Definition: Develops and maintains a mindset that is open, curious, flexible, and client-centered.

B. Co-Creating the Relationship

3. Establishes and Maintains Agreements

Definition: Partners with the client and relevant stakeholders to create clear agreements about the coaching relationship, process, plans and goals. Establishes agreements for the overall coaching engagement as well as those for each coaching session.

4. Cultivates Trust and Safety

Definition: Partners with the client to create a safe, supportive environment that allows the client to share freely. Maintains a relationship of mutual respect and trust.

5. Maintains Presence

Definition: Is fully conscious and present with the client, employing a style that is open, flexible, and confident.

C. Communicating Effectively

6. Listens Actively

Definition: Focuses on what the client is and is not saying to fully understand what is being communicated in the context of the client systems and to support client self-expression.

---

108. ICF, "ICF Core Competencies."

7. Evokes Awareness

Definition: Facilitates client insight and learning by using tools and techniques such as powerful questioning, silence, metaphor, or analogy.

D. Cultivating Learning and Growth

8. Facilitates Client Growth

Definition: Partners with the client to transform learning and insight into action. Promotes client autonomy in the process.

WHAT IS CHRISTIAN COACHING?

Continuing with the theme of the question "what does this mean?" an essential question that needs to be explored is: what does it mean to utilize coaching within the Church, especially applied to vocational discipleship? In this section, I will explore what Christian coaching is, and its application for discipling believers in discovering and living out their calling in Christ. A helpful definition for understanding what Christian coaching is comes again from Collins when he puts a twist on his previous definition of coaching as applied to a faith context:

> Christian coaching is the practice of guiding and enabling individuals or groups to move from where they are to where God wants them to be. Human goals, dreams, aspirations, and gifts are not discounted, as these often come from God. But Christian coaches encourage others to find God's vision for their lives and to move from following their own agendas to pursuing God's purposes.[109]

In many ways, Christian coaching is very similar to coaching that is developed outside of the church, with a few key differences. Collins highlights a significant difference when he states that instead of coaching believers to pursue their will and purpose in life, a Christian coach works with the PBC to pursue God's will and purposes for their life. Logan and Carlton succinctly sum up this emphasis on empowering believers to seek God's will and purpose through coaching when they state, "Find out what God wants you to do and do it. The role of a coach is simply to help them find out what that looks like for him or her and then help that person figure out ways

---

109. Collins, *Christian Coaching*, 23.

to do it."[110] In regards to Luther's teaching on vocation, this would be aiding a coachee to assess who their neighbors are in their various stations of life, and exploring what it would look like to love and serve them uniquely within those contexts with the gifts and talents that are at the believer's disposal.

Collins's definition addresses how Christian coaching can help believers better discern and live out their vertical calling in Christ in their horizontal callings in life. Webb highlights this potential for vocational coaching when he writes, "Coaching is an ongoing intentional conversation that empowers a person or group to fully live out God's calling."[111] In a qualitative study entitled "Examining How the Beliefs of Christian Coaches Impact Their Coaching Practice," Paul Duncan explores how the fundamental faith convictions of Christian coaches influence their coaching with others when he explains,

> All of the coaches commented on the fact that they believed that God has a plan or purpose for everyone and that this meta-narrative in particular helps them to relax in the coaching environment. Illustrative of this were quotes such as "Every human being was created in order or with a calling on their life or a destiny you could call it." And again "... that God has planted in them, of a life vision they are meant to discover and to fulfill."[112]

While the discernment of calling can occur through many different means, coaching can be an intentional process to help believers better discern what God is trying to say to them and what it means to live that out in life.[113]

Another definition that is useful in understanding Christian coaching's distinctive nature is when Miller and Hall state, "Christian coaching is a focused Christ-centered relationship that cultivates a person's sustained growth and action."[114] Breaking down their definition, in their view, Christian coaching has the following features. It is a focused relationship that is purposeful. It is also Christ-centered, for, without Christ present, there is no Christian coaching. That doesn't mean the PBC has to be a Christian, but the coach does. However, Christian coaches make an assumption that God is already at work in someone's life, for believers and unbelievers alike,

---

110. Logan and Carlton, *Coaching 101*, 23.
111. Webb, *COACH Model*, 28.
112. Duncan, "Examining," 34–35.
113. Webb, *COACH Model*, 30.
114. Miller and Hall, *Coaching for Christian Leaders*, 10.

before coaching begins.[115] In addition to God's presence, Christian coaching is intended to cultivate the coachee's sustained growth and action.[116] This definition of Miller and Hall highlights a vital conviction that Christian coaches bring to the coaching conversation; that there are three present in the coaching relationship—the coach, the PBC, and God.[117]

It is God working through the Holy Spirit's power, who is the crucial player in the coaching relationship.[118] Miller and Hall discuss the Holy Spirit's pivotal role in the coaching relationship when they explain, "The Holy Spirit is a vital participant in the Christian coaching relationship! The Christian coach brings a strong belief that the person being coached, with the help of the Holy Spirit, can discover the solutions that will move that person forward."[119] It is the Holy Spirit who is the real Paraclete, not the coach, and he has the power to truly transform lives for now and for eternity.[120] As such, the coach's role is to help their clients listen and rely on the Holy Spirit's leading in their lives.[121] Yes, a Christian coach works with the PBC to find solutions for what they are seeking help with, through coaching. However, the coach also helps the coachee rely on God to discover those solutions as well. Ultimately, in Collins's view, "For the Christian coach, God—not human ingenuity—is at the core of his or her being, and God is the guide for all coaching work."[122]

One last definition that adds a great deal of value in understanding how Christian coaching is similar and distinct from coaching, as understood in a secular sense, comes from Jane Creswell, when she shares the following equation: "Christ's Vision and Mission + Scriptural Principles + Christ's Presence + High Standard of Excellence as Trained Coach = CHRISTIAN COACHING."[123] Here is a basis for understanding how Christian coaching can be valuable for helping believers discern and live out their vocation in Christ in their daily areas of responsibility in life. A Christian coach trains to meet the highest standards of coaching excellence, as outlined by groups

---

115. Webb, *COACH Model*, 31.
116. Miller and Hall, *Coaching for Christian Leaders*, 12.
117. Creswell, *Christ-Centered Coaching*, 7.
118. Miller and Hall, *Coaching for Christian Leaders*, 75.
119. Miller, *Coaching for Christian Leaders*, 76.
120. Hall et al., *Faith Coaching*, 7.
121. Miller and Hall, *Coaching for Christian Leaders*, 76.
122. Collins, *Christian Coaching*, 24.
123. Creswell, *Christ-Centered Coaching*, 14.

like the ICF and others. However, the Christian coach will distinctly seek to connect the PBC's vision and mission for their lives to Christ's vision and purpose for their lives and the world. The Christian coach also seeks to apply Scripture to how they carry out their coaching practice and connect the coachee to the Word so that they can better discern God's will for their life and be empowered by the Holy Spirit. Finally, a Christian coach trusts Jesus' promise of his presence in the coaching relationship, working through the coach as a mask, as Luther teaches in his theological understanding of vocation.

In addition to these helpful definitions regarding the nature of Christian coaching, some other aspects need to be examined. First, it is vital to understand the relationship between coaching and discipleship. In his view, Collins does not see coaching as discipleship.[124] He explains this view when he states, "Coaching is not *primarily* about helping people grow spiritually, even though that may be a part of some coaching. In contrast, coaching is about career development, getting unstuck, developing and reaching corporate and personal goals, managing conflict, getting through life transitions, clarifying visions, building better relationships. I do not see this as the main goal of discipleship."[125] However, when seen through Luther's teaching on vocation, coaching can be a powerful tool for personalized vocational discipleship. Christian coaching can not only help believers grow in their faith and identity in Christ but can also be used to empower them to live out their faith by loving and serving their neighbors in their various areas of responsibility. As Hall notes, faith coaching focuses on the "whole" of life, not only the "part" that we sometimes place in the faith compartment. Ultimately, for a Christian coach, they seek to empower believers to live an integrated faith and life in line with God's vision for life.[126]

Christian coaching is also distinctive in meeting people where they are in their faith journey rather than offering them a one-size-fits-all approach to discipleship. Creswell explains that Christian coaches need to recognize that people are at different places in their faith journey when she states, "Coaching honors the differences in people, in their ways of thinking and in their choice of next steps. It can be a tool that allows people to be at different levels of their faith journey and still help them make progress

---

124. Collins, *Christian Coaching*, 20.
125. Collins, *Christian Coaching*, 20.
126. Hall et al., *Faith Coaching*, 91.

along the way."[127] Given this reality, coaching is individualized for believers wherever they are on faith's journey as they travel through a life of vocation on their way to eternity. As Luther reminds us in regards to the journey of faith for believers as they live a life of vocation, "This life is not righteous, but growth in righteousness; it is not health, but healing; not being, but becoming; not rest, but exercise; we are not yet what we shall be, but we are growing toward it; the process is not yet finished, but it is going on; this is not the end, but it is the road; all does not yet gleam in glory, but all is being purified."[128] Through faith in one's vertical relationship with Christ, a believer is made right in the sight of God by grace and in their horizontal relationships in life, they are to grow in living that calling rightly with their neighbors.

The last area to examine in Christian coaching is the understanding of the basic nature of humanity. One assumption that is made in the wider world of coaching is that people are basically whole. As one of the four cornerstones of coaching, the authors of *Co-Active Coaching* make the following assumption: "We start with this assertion: people are, by their very nature, creative, resourceful and whole."[129] While Christian coaching can agree with the assumption that people are, by nature, creative and resourceful, oftentimes able to come up with their own solutions, it cannot accept that people are basically whole. In Rom 3:23 (NIV) we hear from Paul, "For all have sinned and fall short of the glory of God." Sin impacts every level of one's being and life and, as such, humanity is not whole but broken. Miller and Hall counter this notion that people are basically whole when they write, "When people become acquainted with coaching, one common misconception is that 'all of the resources for a whole life lie within the person.' If this were true, everyone could be their own 'savior,' and no one would need Jesus, except perhaps to serve as teacher or as role model."[130] At the end of the day, Christian coaches recognize all are in need of a Savior, Jesus, and point people to him when their plans and lives don't work out in the way they envisioned or intended.

---

127. Creswell, *Coaching for Excellence*, 247.
128. Luther, "Defense and Explanation," 24.
129. Kimsey-House et al., *Co-Active Coaching*, 3.
130. Miller and Hall, *Coaching for Christian Leaders*, 119.

DEFINITION OF VOCATIONAL COACHING

Given all of these definitions and understandings of coaching that I have referenced, both from the secular arena and its use within the Church, it is essential that I define what vocational coaching is. I define vocational coaching within a Christian context as empowering believers to discover and live out their authentic calling in Christ in their areas of responsibility in life for greater kingdom impact. This approach to vocational coaching seeks to assist the PBC in creating awareness around both their ultimate identity in their vertical relationship in Christ and discovering their unique identity as part of God's workmanship and design in their lives to maximize their kingdom potential (ultimate identity + unique identity = authentic identity). Vocational coaching also seeks to empower a believer to grow as a disciple of Jesus holistically in their heart, soul, mind, and body. Then, serving as a creative think-partner, the coach works with their coachee to develop a vision for how to more intentionally live out their authentic calling in Christ for greater impact in their horizontal relationships by loving and serving their neighbors in their stations of family, church, work life, and society. The coach does this by assisting the coachee in aligning their passions and values in life with God's will for the world as seen through Luther's teaching on vocation, developing goals and strategies to practically live that out, and helping them overcome obstacles and objections while providing encouragement, support, and gospel accountability along the way.

HOW CAN COACHING MAKE AN IMPACT?

With this understanding of the nature and development of the field of coaching, it becomes imperative to ask again the question "What does this mean?" In particular, what does coaching mean in practical terms regarding the kind of impact it can have on those who seek out and receive coaching? How does coaching help individuals navigate both the challenges and opportunities that this ever-changing world has to offer? How can people find meaning and purpose in life, especially in this post-church and post-Christian culture, where so much of life seems meaningless? How can someone make an impact beyond themselves to make their community and world a better place? How can one not only survive but thrive in life? And where does one's puzzle piece fit within the grand jigsaw puzzle of life?

These are but a few of the questions that coaching can help people not only explore but begin to answer.

Navigating Adaptive Challenges

As previously noted, coaching developed in response to many of the adaptive challenges that individuals and organizations were experiencing as a result of the accelerating speed of change in our world. In an article entitled "Context of Coaching," Frederick Hudson addresses the unique context coaching was born from when he writes,

> Very few professions have been born in a change-dominated world. Most professionals (teachers, physicians, lawyers, psychologists, and others) function with a set of core skills and concepts that they keep repeating throughout their linear careers. The coaching field emerged as a field to facilitate change and development as its central functions.[131]

Coaching, in its essence, is about helping navigate and facilitate change. Hudson explains how, for much of the twentieth century, the world in the West was relatively dependable and predictable.[132] As such, the lives of many reflected the nature of that continuity. However, he notes how life currently is more complicated and tentative. Hudson describes how there is only one constant now that can be depended upon when he states, "The central force that shapes our consciousness today is change, change, change—coming at us from every direction, and in every aspect of our lives."[133] In the equation of life, change seems to be a constant that needs to be factored in.

In an article written by Pam McLean on "A Developmental Perspective in Coaching," she explains the need to navigate this constant condition of change in life when she states,

> Life today breeds endless change and our ability to map the way, understanding an ongoing and normative change process that is always present in our lives allows us to make far more intentional choices. Simply put, change is a ubiquitous force in today's world. Leaders and organizations have only a handful of choices in this new terrain—to react, resist, or leverage the inevitable change as

---

131. Hudson, "Context of Coaching," 14.
132. Hudson, "Context of Coaching," 6.
133. Hudson, "Context of Coaching," 6.

an opportunity for development—allowing us to reinvent ourselves and our systems as we remain engaged, agile and vibrant.[134]

Everyone experiences change at all stages of life, for life is now defined by change. Hudson highlights one example of how, in their lifetime, today's typical college graduate will have six to eight different careers.[135] Change is now an ever-present reality in modern life in the Western context. Many people's perception now has shifted from a world that is orderly and stable to one that is disorderly and change-driven.[136]

Hudson describes four helpful paradigm shifts that coaches can help individuals adjust to in their personal lives or in leading their organizations.[137] The first shift is from "the linear rule," where life gets better and better, to "the cyclical rule," where life becomes measured in cycles and chapters of change, not linear accomplishments. The second shift is from "the steady-state rule," where, if one works hard, they hit a plateau of security and happiness in life, to "the continuous change rule," where process, not progress, defines life. A third shift is "the learning rule," where children and young people learn and then launch into their adult life where there is very little reason to learn more, to "the learning is for everyone rule," where constant change requires continuous learning and training throughout one's lifetime. Each of these will require coaches to help individuals make the necessary mental shifts to adapt effectively to this constant state of change.

There is a fourth paradigm shift that is especially important for Christian coaches to keep in mind as they work with believers in helping them to discover and live out their calling in Christ in all of their callings in life. This is the shift from "the outside-in rule" to "the inside-out rule." In regards to "the outside-in rule," Hudson explains,

> This rule said our personal lives are defined and determined by the directives of the society around us. From this point of view, the boxes of life around us shape and determine our personal choices. Nobody talked about "life planning" or "coaching" because people thought their lives were already planned and secured by the larger society.[138]

---

134. McLean, "Developmental Perspective," 31.
135. Hudson, *Handbook of Coaching*, 7.
136. Hudson, "Context of Coaching," 6–7.
137. Hudson, "Context of Coaching," 9.
138. Hudson, "Context of Coaching," 12–13.

Hudson defines these "boxes of life" as family, global roles and citizenship, community and church, work and career, and volunteer groups and associations. These align well with Luther's stations of life—church, family, work, and society. Many could find their identity in these various boxes or stations in generations past, along with happiness, stability, and fulfillment.

However, according to Hudson, these changing times, with many of the adaptive challenges people face today, calls for an "inside-out" approach to life. He goes on to argue for this approach when he explains,

> To succeed as human beings in the twenty-first century, we need to be on-purpose persons, shaping our actions in the world with our inner beliefs. Our many roles as an adult—at work, home, play, community and the rest—are meant to be extensions of our inner selves—our core values.[139]

Because there are so many adaptive challenges and changes today, there needs to be something else to anchor one's identity and security in life than these outward "boxes." Vocational coaching can be a powerful tool to empower believers to live their lives from the inside-out, not the outside-in. Coaches can guide believers to discover their ultimate identity in their vertical relationship with Jesus. From there can come inside beliefs and values that influence how they live out their horizontal calling in their various areas of responsibilities in life, no matter how much change and challenge they experience. Hudson suggests that coaches can help individuals develop their "gyroscopes," which are their identity and values, that can keep them balanced amid challenges and their "radar" to analyze their best choices to make in navigating an ever-changing environment.[140] From this inside-out coaching approach, a coach can help clients more effectively live out their calling in Christ in the various systems which gives life its context.[141]

Coaching Change

Coaching is a comprehensive process that can help individuals navigate the change they face in their lives, both externally and internally. Coaching can also be a process to help people achieve the change they desire. According to Collins, "The work of coaches is all about change. These are

139. Hudson, "Context of Coaching," 12–13.
140. Hudson, "Context of Coaching," 17.
141. Hudson, *Handbook of Coaching*, 143.

people who encourage, guide, and walk with those who want their lives to be different."[142] A coach serves the PBC as a change assistant and change initiator.[143] Coaching is about helping people make changes, even when it is uncomfortable to do so. However, while coaches are change agents, according to Bacon and Voss, "Change is the client's responsibility, and no change will occur no matter how helpful or brilliant the coach is if the client isn't able to make it happen."[144] A coach can guide the coachee through a self-discovery process, helping them recognize their need for change and support them in making that transition in their lives. However, it is ultimately up to the client to make change happen.

According to Bacon and Voss, "Awareness is the necessary foundation for change and development to occur. The ability to seek truth and the willingness to embrace it requires courage."[145] Unfortunately, fear can often keep both individuals and organizations in their comfort zones even when the need for change is evident.[146] There is a saying that goes "People don't change when they see the light; it is when they feel the heat." While some do indeed change when they see the light, so many do not. It is often when someone feels the heat that they seek the assistance of a coach. The urgency to change must be greater than their fear for change to happen.[147] It may take believing in something greater than themselves, like faith in God, for change to occur.[148] For real, lasting change to take place, it may mean some rewiring in one's thought patterns, which becomes harder the older people get, so that new habits can emerge.[149] As such, coaches need to remember that change is a process, not an event.

In his book *Change or Die* Alan Deutschman examines why so few people change in life, like when they receive news from their doctor that they need to change their lifestyle, or they will indeed die. He describes three "F's" that rarely, if ever, create change: "Facts, Fear, and Force."[150] Instead, he shares three "R's" that are proven to help produce a change in

---

142. Collins, *Christian Coaching*, 51.
143. Collins, *Christian Coaching*, 52.
144. Bacon and Voss, *Adaptive Coaching*, 247.
145. Bacon and Voss, *Adaptive Coaching*, 249.
146. Bacon and Voss, *Adaptive Coaching*, 244.
147. Bacon and Voss, *Adaptive Coaching*, 252.
148. Bacon and Voss, *Adaptive Coaching*, 254.
149. Bacon and Voss, *Adaptive Coaching*, 246–47.
150. Deutschman, *Change or Die*, 58.

people: "Relate, Repeat, and Reframe."[151] Coaches can provide their clients with all three of these "R's." First, a coach is someone the coachee can "relate" to who inspires hope that change is possible through a trusted relationship. Second, the coach works with the PBC to "repeat" new behaviors and skills that will affect desired change. Finally, the coach helps the client "reframe" to learn new ways of thinking about their situation in life. Ultimately, coaching can help individuals build the awareness, commitment, practice, and accountability they need to navigate change outwardly and create change inwardly as well.[152]

One of the most valuable ways coaches can serve their clients is by walking along with them through times of change and transition. Auerbach addresses this vital role coaches fulfill for those they coach when he states,

> Often, an important aspect of personal coaching is aiding a client in transition. Coaches frequently are involved in helping people move from one phase of development to another. . . . The coach can aid clients by framing some life experiences as rites of passage and supporting them appropriately during the transition.[153]

Loss of family, job, personal trials, death of a loved one, betrayal of a friend, etc. can all lead to a time of transition in life. And with these transitions can come a loss of identity. In an academic paper on "Coaching Needs to Differ before and after the Transition to Retirement," Tessa Dodwell notes that everyone in her study who went through a transition into retirement struggled with a loss of identity.[154] One of the most significant struggles that those who go through a job loss or retirement experience during times of transition is answering the question "Who am I?" Coaches can assist their clients going through this change and transition to connect to a new identity through inside-out coaching. This is especially true for Christian coaches as they help connect believers to their ultimate identity vertically as a baptized child of God through faith in Christ. A coach can also assist the PBC with navigating either mini-transitions or major life transitions in developing a game plan, connecting with friends, networking, exploring new opportunities, and retooling with the skills and knowledge they will need.[155]

---

151. Deutschman, *Change or Die*, 14–15.
152. Bacon and Voss, *Adaptive Coaching*, 248.
153. Auerbach, *Personal and Executive Coaching*, 12–13.
154. Dodwell, "Coaching Needs to Differ," 111.
155. Auerbach, *Personal and Executive Coaching*, 157.

Awareness and Action

Ultimately, coaching is about two things—creating awareness and forwarding action. Regarding this unique distinction and value that coaching offers, Miller and Hall write, "Both discovery and action are vital to the coaching process."[156] A coach works with the coachee to bring awareness of those things they already know, but are unaware that they know, and take action on the goals and vision they have set for themselves.[157] According to Hall, Copper, and McElveen, coaching aims to create cognitive and behavioral change:

> Finally, coaching leads to both cognitive change and behavioral change. Behavioral and cognitive are just fancy ways of saying "how we act" and "how we think." Modern Western approaches to faith development tend to focus on one or the other, but not both. . . . Coaching helps bridge the cognitive/behavioral divide by linking our values, thoughts, and actions so that our thoughts and actions align and flow from the same source.[158]

It is the combination of aligning both learning and action together that creates change in the PBC.[159] Tony Stoltzfus, in his book *Leadership Coaching*, discusses how a coach helps their client by pushing them to think in ways they haven't done before and then taking responsibility for the things they have decided to do.[160] As Whitmore notes, "Building AWARENESS and RESPONSIBILITY is the essence of good coaching."[161]

Deepening Awareness

Before coaching someone to act, deepening their awareness is essential. Whitmore affirms this need to create awareness in the PBC when he states, "The first key element of coaching is awareness, which is the product of focused attention, concentration, and clarity."[162] Coaches serve as "awareness raisers." They don't need to experience or be experts in an area to be an

---

156. Miller and Hall, *Coaching for Christian Leaders*, 33.
157. Hall et al., *Faith Coaching*, 16.
158. Hall et al., *Faith Coaching*, 40.
159. Kimsey-House et al., *Co-Active Coaching*, 7.
160. Stoltzfus, *Leadership Coaching*, 7.
161. Whitmore, *Coaching for Performance*, 33.
162. Whitmore, *Coaching for Performance*, 34.

effective coach. They just have to be skilled in raising awareness in others.[163] Again, Whitmore highlights that the coach's goal is to make the client dig deep to create new levels of awareness when he explains,

> If a coach only asks questions and receives answers from the normal level of consciousness, he may be helping the coachee to structure his thoughts, but he is not probing to new or deeper levels of awareness. When the coachee has to stop to think before responding, maybe raising his eyes to do so, awareness is being raised. The coachee is having to plumb new depths of his consciousness to retrieve the information. It is as if he is delving into his inner filing cabinet to find the answer. Once found, this new awareness becomes conscious, and the coachee is empowered by it.[164]

The awareness created is not primarily for the coach, but for the PBC. While the new awareness gives the coach ideas where to explore next through the questions they ask, what is most important is that it is the client who understands how they need to move forward with their purpose and goals.[165] Those "a-ha" moments of discovery are golden for both the coach and the coachee because that new knowledge is empowering.[166]

When a coach seeks to deepen the PBC's awareness, it can be understood in terms of "idea mining."[167] In their book, *Coaching That Counts*, Dianna Anderson and Merrill Anderson explain this idea when it comes to deepening awareness when writing,

> Clients reflect on their experiences, gain insight, and translate their insights into action plans that lead to next experiences. This process continues until clients achieve the desired outcome. In transformational coaching, the coaches guide their clients to establish this pattern of mining experiences for insight.[168]

They note that the real power comes when one independent idea is combined with another separate idea creating new insight, fresh inspiration, and "a-ha" moments of new possibility.[169] Creswell also notes that the brain

---

163. Whitmore, *Coaching for Performance*, 42.
164. Whitmore, *Coaching for Performance*, 69.
165. Whitmore, *Coaching for Performance*, 46.
166. Creswell, *Christ-Centered Coaching*, 81.
167. Creswell, *Coaching for Excellence*, 12.
168. Anderson and Anderson, *Coaching That Counts*, 21.
169. Anderson and Anderson, *Coaching That Counts*, 25.

has a "use it or lose it" system of connections.[170] As such, idea mining helps move information from short-term memory into long-term memory, not only when the information is accessed but also when it is put into action.

A valuable coaching concept when it comes to the idea of deepening awareness in individuals, especially in considering how to coach believers to discover and live out their calling in Christ, is Creswell's "Knowledge Model."[171] This knowledge model describes two different ways to increase awareness.

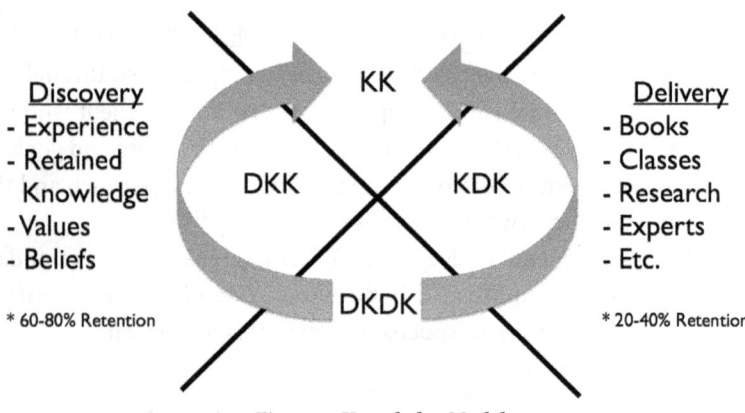

Figure 3. Knowledge Model

KK = *Know* what you *know*
DKK = *Didn't know* what you *knew*
KDK = *Know* what you *don't know*
DKDK = *Don't know* what you *don't know*

The right side of the model is a delivery approach that seeks to create awareness through external sources like seminars, books, classes, etc. As we think of the methods the church uses to disciple believers in the past, it typically utilizes a delivery approach using sermons, Bible studies, training, seminars, etc. Through a delivery approach, the average person retains 20–40 percent of what is learned.[172] However, on the left side of the model

170. Creswell, *Christ-Centered Coaching*, 83.
171. Creswell, *Christ-Centered Coaching*, 78–80.
172. Creswell, *Christ-Centered Coaching*, 80.

is a discovery approach that is represented by coaching. Instead of utilizing external means (delivery) to create awareness, it focuses on an internal pathway (discovery) of tapping into the coachee's retained knowledge, experiences, values, and beliefs. Creswell explains, "A coach can help ask discovery questions to help you 'connect the dots' for new learning. The coach helps you discover those internal resources. A coach helps you look inside yourself for the answers."[173] Via a discovery approach, knowledge uncovered through internal resources is retained at 60–80 percent.[174]

In explaining this knowledge model, Creswell advocates that the best coaches start by creating awareness of what is already inside the PBC's brain through a discovery approach.[175] A coach then helps the client move in a targeted way to a delivery approach, identify classes, seminars, and books that will fill in the gaps in their knowledge. She adds, "Even when you must add new external learning, you will want to take the internal path first. If you explore your internal resources, you can more precisely determine the gaps in what you need to know and target external learning to meet your exact needs."[176] Miller and Hall argue that effective coaching helps individuals benefit from internal and external sources of knowledge to deepen their awareness and identify what they are missing.[177]

However, another approach to consider is starting with a delivery approach, in the form of a workshop or training, and then adding coaching as a follow-up to deepen the awareness of participants of what they have just learned, and furthering their action by applying this new learning in personal and practical ways to their life. During the 2021 International Positive Psychology Association (IPPA) "Evidence in Action" online conference, Dr. Suzy Green, with The Positivity Institute, gave a presentation on "Positive Psychology Coaching" in which she shared, "A training session alone will not be sufficient, but using and complementing that training session with a coaching approach, whether that is self-coaching, co-coaching peers, or formal professional coaching, has the capacity to enhance learning retention and transfer of training."[178] This discovery and delivery approach, whichever side of the knowledge model one begins with, could be

---

173. Creswell, *Christ-Centered Coaching*, 79.
174. Creswell, *Christ-Centered Coaching*, 80.
175. Creswell, *Christ-Centered Coaching*, 81.
176. Creswell, *Christ-Centered Coaching*, 80.
177. Miller and Hall, *Coaching for Christian Leaders*, 119.
178. Green, "Positive Psychology Coaching."

a powerful one-two process to personally disciple believers to deepen their awareness of their calling in Christ as they seek to live out their vocations in their daily life.

The distinctiveness of Christian coaching versus a broader understanding of coaching when it comes to creating awareness is that the coach is helping the PBC tap into what they already know as well as tapping into what God and others know to come up with the answers they need.[179] Sometimes, what is required to deepen awareness for a client is not another class or training but for individuals, with the help of a coach, to tap into the retained knowledge of God's Word that they already have within them. While some may indeed need to pursue a delivery pathway to deepen their awareness of God's Word due to the growing level of biblical illiteracy in our culture today, there are others for whom taking a discovery path will be appropriate and beneficial.

When it comes to believers discerning their vocation, Collins also notes, "God guides in various ways, but most of us don't find our life missions until we are aware of our values, passions, strengths, and visions."[180] These are all topics that Christian coaches are trained to explore with those they coach to discover and live out their calling in life. Collins highlights these aspects that Christian coaches can help believers to explore and create awareness in regards to their vocation: their current circumstances, worldviews, beliefs, personality, and spiritual gifts.[181] One important question that a Christian coach can help their coachee discern, when it comes to vocation, is "Who is my neighbor and how best can I serve them with the gifts God has given to me?"

Unlocking Untapped Potential

An aspect of deepening awareness that is especially important in coaching is unlocking a person's untapped potential. Auerbach highlights this essential focus of coaching when he explains, "Coaching focuses on helping people unleash their potential."[182] Creating awareness around one's untapped potential is also a significant focus of Christian coaching. Creswell postulates the impact coaching can have to this end in the lives of believers in the church

---

179. Miller and Hall, *Coaching for Christian Leaders*, 18.
180. Collins, *Christian Coaching*, 190.
181. Collins, *Christian Coaching*, 135.
182. Auerbach, *Personal and Executive Coaching*, 3.

when she asks, "What if lay people were to move from the 'not-all' to the 'all' state? What if their untapped potential could be harnessed and used in kingdom ministry? What if they could become motivated, enthusiastic, totally committed?"[183] There is empowerment that comes in a person's life when they realize their potential. Ultimately, an essential goal of coaching with believers is to help them put their potential to work in their callings in life by assisting them in identifying their God-given strengths.[184] Again, Creswell explains what is meant by "strengths" when she elaborates, "Strengths are talents, gifts, abilities, personality preferences, and cognitive preferences."[185]

In coaching, there are many excellent formalized assessment tools that can help coachees begin to create awareness of one's God-given gifts and talents; each distinctively focused on a different aspect of their workmanship and design. The MBTI (Myers-Briggs) helps individuals understand their personality in regards to their relationship with themselves, others, and life.[186] There is also the VIA (Values in Action) that helps identify one's character strengths and values.[187] There are emotional intelligence assessments like the EQ-i 2.0.[188] Gallup's BP10® (Builder Profile) assesses for entrepreneurial talent.[189] There are countless other assessment tools like the CPI (California Psychological Inventory) that highlight one's personality and behavior, as well as the FIRO-B (Fundamental Interpersonal Relations Orientation-Behavior), which assesses how a client's personal needs affect their behavior toward other people.[190] There are also more informal assessment tools like Auerbach's "Values Clarification Exercise."[191] Each are effective for creating awareness and facilitating growth in those who receive coaching. Of all the assessment tools that I have utilized in my coaching, the one that resonates most with my clients, as well as effectively identifies some of an individual's natural God-given talents, is the CliftonStrengths®[192]

---

183. Creswell, *Christ-Centered Coaching*, 5.
184. Creswell, *Christ-Centered Coaching*, 15–16.
185. Creswell, *Christ-Centered Coaching*, 40.
186. Myers, *Introduction to Type*, 1–2.
187. Seligman, *Flourish*, 38–40.
188. Stein and Book, *EQ Edge*, 21.
189. Clifton and Badal, *Born to Build*, 167.
190. Auerbach, *Personal and Executive Coaching*, 142–43.
191. Auerbach, *Personal and Executive Coaching*, 245.
192. Gallup®, CliftonStrengths® and the CliftonStrengths 34 Themes of Talent are trademarks of Gallup, Inc. All rights reserved.

assessment (a.k.a. StrengthsFinder), which I will address more in depth in chapter 4.

Forwarding Action

After deepening awareness, the next step in the coaching process is forwarding action. Auerbach elaborates on what forwarding action is about in coaching when he explains, "'Forwarding the action' is coaching jargon for the coach's interventions that facilitate clients' committing to action steps to bring them closer to the stated outcomes of the coaching agenda."[193] Coaching is focused on action. If there is no action, there is no coaching.[194] According to Creswell, "Coaching always has action as its goal."[195] Coaches know how to help their clients identify and take the necessary action to achieve their objectives. However, action for action's sake is not the goal of coaching. It is about taking the right action to effect the desired change. Hall, Copper, and McElveen note that the action a person takes in a coaching relationship flows from the awareness that the coach helps create: "We guide others to consider reality, possibilities, barriers, opportunities, and outcomes. The actions taken by the person being coached are born out of new levels of understanding fostered by the coaching relationship."[196]

Designing action is where the rubber meets the road in coaching, according to Hall, Copper, and McElveen.[197] However, the action can't just be another thing to add to one's to-do list. In Hall et al.'s view, "Meaningful action is not just more action, but the right or best action to achieve the desired outcome on the issue of focus. Meaningful action leads to the transformation that moves the PBC into a preferred future."[198] It starts with creating clear goals that the PBC believes are realistic and attainable.[199] Then, the coach helps the coachee take responsibility for the actions they decide upon. Whitmore highlights the importance of this step of forwarding action in coaching when he writes, "Responsibility is the other key concept or goal of coaching. . . . When we truly accept, choose, or take responsibility

---

193. Auerbach, *Personal and Executive Coaching*, 134.
194. Creswell, *Coaching for Excellence*, 19.
195. Creswell, *Coaching for Excellence*, 6.
196. Hall et al., *Faith Coaching*, 196.
197. Hall et al., *Faith Coaching*, 130.
198. Hall et al., *Faith Coaching*, 130.
199. Hudson, *Handbook of Coaching*, 20.

for our thoughts and actions, our commitment to them rises and so does our performance."[200] The importance of a client taking responsibility for following through on the action they decide upon is why advice-giving is avoided in coaching.[201] If a client takes the coach's advice, and it doesn't work out, it is easy to blame the coach rather than take responsibility that, perhaps, the outcome was due to the coachee's lack of ownership for the action taken.

Transformational Coaching

As much as you can't have coaching without doing, one's being is also a primary focus of coaching. Hudson describes a coach's role regarding working with a client's being and doing when he states, "The two poles of coaching are (1) coaching for *being* and (2) coaching for *performance*. Neither is more or less important; the two are necessary parts of every human being and every coaching task."[202] Auerbach distinguishes coaching prioritized on one's being as transformational coaching.[203] Performance coaching focuses on developing skills and actions as well as developing strategic goals and action plans. Alternatively, transformational coaching focuses on changes in perspectives, values, potential, and future direction. Anderson and Anderson argue that coaches who focus solely on doing, and not being, miss the full transformational power of coaching.[204] Hudson notes that many seek out coaching to work on performance issues; however, as the coaching relationship develops, transformational coaching topics emerge.[205] And from this exploration of coaching focused on "being," new outward actions aimed at "doing" begin to develop. To this point, Hargrove asserts, "Our way of being is usually the source of intended results."[206]

A valuable framework for thinking about transformational coaching comes from Robert Hargrove's "Triple Loop Learning Model."[207] He describes these three loops of learning when he explains,

200. Whitmore, *Coaching for Performance*, 37.
201. Whitmore, *Coaching for Performance*, 38.
202. Hudson, *Handbook of Coaching*, 20.
203. Auerbach, *Personal and Executive Coaching*, 29.
204. Anderson and Anderson, *Coaching That Counts*, 20.
205. Hudson, *Handbook of Coaching*, 20.
206. Hargrove, *Masterful Coaching*, 144.
207. Hargrove, *Masterful Coaching*, 115.

> A Masterful Coach gets to the source of the breakdown and makes use of one or more of three learning loops: triple loop—altering people's way of being; double loop—altering people's mental models and thereby their thinking and actions; and single loop—tips and techniques.[208]

Each learning loop reflects the type of questions that a coach would ask the PBC, each with a distinct purpose. The first loop of questions focuses on the client's actions. However, while helpful to a point, there are times when actions fail and new strategies are needed, leading to the second loop of questions focused on the coachee's thinking. New ways of thinking also can be valuable to achieve the PBC's goals and objectives when actions fail. However, there are times that individuals need to be different, not just think or act differently, leading to the third loop of learning focusing on one's being. Coaching people at the level of their being can also lead to transformed thinking and action. Hargrove explains this transformational process in coaching when he writes, "Transformation requires intervening in who people are being (triple loop), which in turn influences their thinking (double loop) and behavior (single loop)."[209] Coaches can assist their clients in this transformation process to become the people they need to be to effectively live out their calling in Christ in their daily areas of responsibilities in life.

Transformational coaching is also known as spiritual coaching.[210] It is transformation that spiritual coaching seeks after that is the ultimate goal of Christian coaches, where their clients not only have changed thoughts and actions but they are different at the core of their being.[211] In his book *Jesus Asked* Conrad Gempf examines the parables and questions of Jesus. He explains that, like his parables, Jesus' questions served as a wedge, moving one either toward Jesus and the kingdom or away from him, but would never leave a person where they were before.[212] Powerful questions asked by Christian coaches can do the same, especially as they trust in the power of the Holy Spirit working through the question. In an article written by Elke Hanssmann "Providing Safe Passage into a Larger Life: Supporting Clients' Transformational Change through Coaching," the Christian coaches

---

208. Hargrove, *Masterful Coaching*, 115.
209. Hargrove, *Masterful Coaching*, 116.
210. Hudson, *Handbook of Coaching*, 20.
211. Collins, *Christian Coaching*, 127.
212. Gempf, *Jesus Asked*, 33–36.

she studied recognized that it was not in their power to transform their clients—that was God's job.[213] Viewed from the lens of Luther's teaching on vocation, as coaches utilize their skills and expertise, they do so as a means through which God does his work of transformation in the life of coachees.

As transformation occurs in a coachee, it is the coach's job to help them integrate their being with their doing so that their beliefs and values are aligned with their thinking and their actions.[214] In their book *Coachbook* William Bergquist and Agnes Mura discuss how spiritual coaching is a discernment process, very much aligned with the goal of deepening awareness.[215] They describe this discernment process as helping the client listen to the right voices in their life when they explain,

> Through this process, a coach encourages and enables her coaching client to more deeply examine and reflect on the various "voices" that speak to him in his ongoing life. The coaching client discerns which messages in his life are aligned with his best interests and the best interests of his family, community and society. With the assistance of his coach, the coaching client also discerns which messages draw him away from these best interests.[216]

A Christian coach serves their coachee well when they can help them slow down, quiet out all the other voices in their life telling them who they should be, and help them listen to the voice of Jesus telling them who they truly are, in their vertical calling, through faith in him by grace. After hearing that voice of Jesus regarding their true identity, the coach works to empower the believer to live that identity out in the best interest of their life (and their neighbor's, horizontally) in their various areas of responsibilities.

Vision and Goals

Coaching can have a lasting impact by working with individuals to create a vision for their lives and develop goals and strategic plans to make that picture of a preferred future a reality. Coaching is about developing a vision

---

213. Hanssmann, "Providing Safe Passage," 32.
214. Auerbach, *Personal and Executive Coaching*, 14.
215. Bergquist and Mura, *Coachbook*, 160.
216. Bergquist and Mura, *Coachbook*, 160.

and goals to effect the desired change in one's life.[217] Collins explains that this change starts with developing a vision:

> A vision is a mental picture of the ideal future. It has to do with what the person wants to accomplish, what he or she would like to have happen, and where the client wants to go. Vision applies to businesses, organizations, churches, families, and people who are building careers.[218]

Most people and organizations need a mental picture of where they are going, which helps them see what is possible and pulls them forward.[219] The vision, though, needs to be based in reality.[220] Coaching does not subscribe to a "Disneyland" view where if one can dream it, then it will come true. One can only be what God has called them to be and to do what he has called them to do.

Miller and Hall highlight how vision is vital in Christian coaching when they explain, "Becoming clear about the future is important in coaching. The Scriptures admonish, 'Where there is no vision, the people perish' Prov 29:18 (KJV). Coaching helps individuals find their God-given vision."[221] Without a vision for their lives, people lose a sense of meaning and purpose, as often happens, for example, with those who retire.[222] Coaches can walk along with people to discover a meaningful vision and purpose for their lives. It is Collins who notes that visions can be created or discovered.[223] Luther's teaching on vocation provides a valuable biblical and theological framework to help individuals discover God's vision for their lives, their neighbors, and the world. Through the use of questions that create awareness, a coach can empower the PBC to seek God's will for their life by encouraging them to envision what could be, and living that calling out with intentionality in their various horizontal vocations.[224]

After a vision is created or discovered, goals are established to give something to the coachee to aim for that helps them turn vision into a

---

217. Collins, *Christian Coaching*, 51.
218. Collins, *Christian Coaching*, 120.
219. Collins, *Christian Coaching*, 171.
220. Collins, *Christian Coaching*, 171.
221. Miller and Hall, *Coaching for Christian Leaders*, 63.
222. Collins, *Christian Coaching*, 190.
223. Collins, *Christian Coaching*, 175.
224. Collins, *Christian Coaching*, 121.

reality. A goal is like a bullseye to aim towards. Auerbach describes the process of turning goals into action when he explains,

> The process of translating goals into actions has three elements, all of which you facilitate as a coach: (1) brainstorming potential relevant actions, (2) considering the pros and cons of each action and selecting the best, most useful action, and (3) aiding in anticipating obstacles and preparing a plan to manage them.[225]

When the client has come up with their own ideas and solutions, explored the potential obstacles and objections, and feels supported and encouraged by their coach, they are ready to realize their goals.[226] It is helpful for a coach to work with their client to develop their goals in terms of SMART goals: Specific, Measurable, Attainable, Relevant, Time-Specific.[227] After establishing their goals, the coach works with the coachee to develop a strategic plan. This strategic plan is a step-by-step process that helps the PBC turn their vision, as well as God's vision, for their life into reality.[228] This is reminiscent of Jesus' caution, as he teaches of the cost of discipleship in Luke 14:28, about building a tower; it is important to first count the cost to make sure it can be completed. Planning is vital for a vision and its goals to be realized, especially when it comes to intentionally living out one's vertical calling in Christ in their horizontal responsibilities in life.

---

225. Auerbach, *Personal and Executive Coaching*, 37.
226. Auerbach, *Personal and Executive Coaching*, 38.
227. Stoltzfus, *Leadership Coaching*, 140–41.
228. Auerbach, *Personal and Executive Coaching*, 162.

4

Setting Up the Coaching Project

RED PILL OR BLUE PILL

It was the fall of 1999, and I was gathered with some classmates from Concordia Seminary in St. Louis, Missouri, at Kaldi's Coffee, just across from the seminary campus. We were taking a coffee break in between classes to discuss the most profound metaphor for preaching we had ever come across, which was the newly released movie *The Matrix*. *The Matrix* had just come out in theaters the previous spring, chronicling the heroic story of Thomas Anderson, also known by his hacker handle Neo, who feels as if something is off in life. On an otherwise unimportant day, he receives a cryptic message that the infamous Morpheus desires to meet with him. During their encounter together, Morpheus describes the matrix to Neo, "The Matrix is the world that has been pulled over your eyes to blind you from the truth." Morpheus explains that no one can be told what the matrix is; they have to see it for themselves. Morpheus then offers Neo two choices, represented by two pills, one blue and one red. If he takes the blue pill, he continues living in the delusion he believes is reality. However, Morpheus explains that if Neo takes the red pill, "You stay in Wonderland, and I show you how deep the rabbit hole goes."

After taking the red pill, Neo awakens to a world in which humanity has been reduced to nothing more than batteries by their machine overlords, who keep them enslaved by networking their minds through a computer-generated virtual reality simulation known as "The Matrix." Upon seeing, for himself, the truth of humanity's plight, Morpheus explains the reason that he freed Neo was because he believes that Neo is the one who will rescue all humanity from their captivity. While filled with doubts, Neo begins training with Morpheus. At one point, after Neo saves one of his teammates, Trinity, from a helicopter that crashes into the side of a building, Morpheus says to Neo, "There is a difference between knowing the path and walking the path."

How true this statement of Morpheus to Neo is. Even in real life, there is a difference between knowing the path and walking the path when it comes to Luther's teaching on vocation. While theologians can explain the essence of what Luther's teaching on vocation is and pastors can preach or teach on it, that does not automatically mean that everyday believers necessarily know how to translate and integrate that knowledge into their personal lives in practical ways. Ultimately, for this teaching of Luther's to truly impact believers' lives and, as a result, the countless lives blessed through them, they can't just be told about this teaching of how they have a calling in Christ to love and serve their neighbors; they have to experience it for themselves. Vocational coaching can be a powerful tool to help empower everyday believers to not only know but begin to walk the path of discovering and more intentionally living out their authentic calling in Christ in their everyday areas of responsibility in life.

CALLED2B COACHING FRAMEWORK

For my project, I am proposing developing and implementing a vocational coaching approach designed to empower everyday believers to discover and live out their authentic calling in Christ, in all of their callings in life, in order to be a greater blessing to their neighbors. Rather than taking a free-range coaching approach where the coachee sets the agenda for the coaching engagement, I will instead utilize a coaching framework focused on deepening the participant's awareness of their calling in Christ, who they have been created and redeemed to be, and then helping them further their action by living out that calling in their various areas of responsibility to more effectively love and serve their neighbors. Who would benefit from participating in this vocational coaching framework? The short answer is anyone seeking clarity on discovering how to translate their faith in Christ into practically living it out in every aspect of their everyday life.

This vocational coaching framework approach will be known as Called2B. The reason for this name, Called2B, is to emphasize the importance that our "being" as believers (faith) must always precede our "doing" (good works). Only after increasing a believer's awareness of their calling in Christ (being) can they properly be empowered to begin to live out their callings in life (doing) in a way that they don't mistakenly think that their doing justifies them before God in their being. As such, this is a "transformational" or "spiritual" coaching approach, as opposed to performance coaching. It is also an "inside-out" coaching approach rather than an "outside-in." Ultimately, Called2B will be focused on helping individuals discover and live out who we have been called to be in Christ for the sake of being used by God to be a greater blessing to others. The Called2B coaching framework consists of three elements (focuses): Identity, Empowerment, and Impact.

Coaching for Authentic Identity—A Believer's Ultimate Identity

The first element of this Called2B vocational coaching framework is Identity—connecting believers to their "authentic" identity in Christ. There are two aspects of a believer's authentic identity which will be explored during this element. The first focus will be coaching participants to gain greater awareness of their "ultimate" identity in Christ. In this exploration of a believer's ultimate identity, the coach seeks to help create awareness for the participant regarding the significance of their identity in their vertical relationship to God through faith in Jesus. As explored in chapter 2, Luther termed this vertical relationship "passive (or alien) righteousness." Again, a key passage of Scripture that highlights this vertical relationship for a believer through which their ultimate identity is found are the words of Paul in Eph 2:8–9 (ESV), "For by grace you have been saved through faith. And this is not your own doing; it is the gift of God, not a result of works, so that no one may boast." As a result of this gift of salvation freely given, each believer is loved, forgiven, holy, and redeemed in Christ alone.

From this vertical relationship, established through faith alone in Jesus and his saving work, believers begin to discern their ultimate identity. One aspect of this ultimate identity is one's baptismal identity, as explained by the apostle Paul in Gal 3:26–27 (NIV), "So in Christ Jesus you are all children of God through faith, for all of you who were baptized into Christ have clothed yourselves with Christ." A believer's ultimate identity is now located in Jesus, through whom one is restored to their original created identity as a "son [or] daughter" of God. Through their vertical relationship to God in Christ, believers are also given a new identity as the "royal priesthood," as we read in 1 Pet 2:9 (ESV), "But you are a chosen race, a royal priesthood, a holy nation, a people for his own possession, that you may proclaim the excellencies of him who called you out of darkness into his marvelous light." Martin Luther highlights the importance of this ultimate identity, revealed in 1 Peter, when he writes, "We are all consecrated priests by baptism, as St. Peter says: 'You are a royal priesthood and a priestly realm' (1 Pet 2:9). The Apocalypse says: 'Thou hast made us to be kings and priests by thy blood' (Rev 5:9–10)."[1]

There is also a collective identity that individual believers are integrated into, being part of the body of Christ. Paul explains this organic imagery of the church that believers are now incorporated into, when he explains in Eph 4:15-16 (NIV), "Instead, speaking the truth in love, we will grow to become in every respect the mature body of him who is the head, that is, Christ. From him the whole body, joined and held together by every supporting ligament, grows and builds itself up in love, as each part does its work." In 1 Corinthians, Paul continues to explain how each believer is incorporated into this body by the work of the Spirit, and freely receive this baptismal identity when he writes, "Just as a body, though one, has many parts, but all its many parts form one body, so it is with Christ. For we were all baptized by one Spirit so as to form one body—whether Jews or Gentiles, slave or free—and we were all given the one Spirit to drink." Not all are gifted as a hand, not all a foot, not all an ear, (1 Cor 12:15–20 NIV); however, each believer is a part of the whole body and has a specific role to play as Paul states in 1 Cor 12:27, "Now you are the body of Christ, and each one of you is a part of it."

Besides helping explore the significance of this ultimate identity that is found freely in one's vertical relationship with God, it is also essential to examine what false identities believers have entrusted themselves to in life that might be undermining the living out of their true identity in Christ. Many things in this life offer believers a sense of identity with the promise of life and meaning attached to them in this horizontal existence. These are seen in everything from the type of car one drives, to the designer clothes one wears, to the brand of computer or phone one purchases, to the kind of coffee one drinks, etc. So many things offer identity in this life and yet fail to deliver on their promise. There are also many good and godly things found in life that God intended to help give one a sense of identity, like one's

---

1. Luther, "Open Letter," 212.

family, for example. However, what happens when one experiences divorce as a child and now finds themselves with a new last name due to remarriage that no longer matches their family history or origin? With the high divorce rate in our nation here in the US, many struggle with the question "who am I?" Or, how lasting is the identity of being a "champion" when one's team wins it all in one season, and with that victory the sense of esteem that identity brings, only to have it lost when that same team fails the next season to meet up to the expectation "what have you done for me lately?"

In coaching believers to increase their awareness of their ultimate identity in Christ, the following are some potential coaching questions to explore with participants:

1. When you were younger, who did you most want to be like and why?
2. Not including your faith, what things, both positive and negative, are informing your identity in your life? What voices are you listening to?
3. How does your identity from these voices inform how you see yourself and navigate life?
4. How would you like to see yourself? How would you like to be different when it comes to your identity?
5. Regarding your spiritual journey, how would you describe your relationship with God right now?
6. How is your relationship with God informing your sense of identity?
7. What is your identity in Christ by grace through faith?
8. Where can you discover the full reality of that identity in Christ?
9. What Bible verses come to mind that speak to your ultimate identity in Christ?
10. How does your identity in Christ change how you see yourself? Your life? Your relationships with others? Your relationship with God?
11. What can you do to daily grow in and remember your identity freely given to you in Jesus?
12. How does your new identity in Christ transform how you live out your various callings in life?
13. How does your collective identity as being a part of the body of Christ impact your view of your service within your church?

14. If we are indeed part of the body of Christ, which part of the body are you?
15. How are you different today as a result of our coaching conversation?
16. What steps can you take to grow in your ultimate identity in Christ daily?

Coaching for Authentic Identity—A Believer's Unique Identity

The next step in this first element of Identity within this vocational coaching framework is to also explore one's "authentic" identity in Christ. A shift happens at this juncture in the coaching process to empower participants to grow in their awareness of their God-given gifting and design. Again, as touched on in chapter 2, this is an exploration of Paul's words in Eph 2:10 (ESV), "For we are his workmanship, created in Christ Jesus for good works, which God prepared beforehand, that we should walk in them." There are good works for which God calls every believer to, not for salvation in their vertical relationship with God but in love and service to our neighbors in their horizontal relationships in life. Some could be considered "general" good works in which no unique gifting is required and all believers are called to do in service to their neighbor. However, there are also "unique" good works that believers are called to do that are discovered by better understanding God's workmanship and design in their lives.

In this step in this vocational coaching framework, participants grow in this awareness of their gifting and design by identifying their unique Divine GPS—gifts, passions, and strengths. As a GPS device helps a driver navigate their car while driving, God has gifted within each believer an internal GPS, metaphorically speaking, that aids them in navigating how to live out their calling in Christ vertically, in all their various areas of responsibility in life horizontally. This internal GPS helps them better understand who they have been created and now redeemed to be in Christ as they seek to love and serve their neighbors. It helps them better understand their natural patterns of thinking, feeling, and behaving. It helps them better discern the areas of life in which they have a particular interest and would best flourish for the sake of serving others vocationally. And it helps them better understand what tools they have in their proverbial tool belt to use as they seek to be a blessing to those around them. There are various assessments that this vocational coaching framework will utilize to aid in this discerning process.

The Gift of Personality

The first aspect of a believer's Divine GPS to be explored is the gift of one's personality. In Ps 139:13–16 (ESV), the psalmist declares how it is God who has formed each one of us within our mother's womb when he writes,

> For you formed my inward parts; you knitted me together in my mother's womb. I praise you, for I am fearfully and wonderfully made. Wonderful are your works; my soul knows it very well. My frame was not hidden from you, when I was being made in secret, intricately woven in the depths of the earth. Your eyes saw my unformed substance; in your book were written, every one of them, the days that were formed for me, when as yet there was none of them.

This workmanship of God was not just one's physical form as part of his creative work but also each aspect of themselves, which also includes the innate parts of their personality. There is also a link in this passage between understanding this workmanship of God in one's life and the days formed for each one of us by God. This is why exploration of one's personality is vital, as it has an impact not only in what one does in their various callings in life but also how they go about their relationships with others.

However, personality is multifaceted. There has been a long-standing question of whether personality is a result of nature or nurture. The answer to this question is yes. There is a part of one's personality that is innate as part of God's design, which can be understood as one's "temperament," and another aspect shaped by engagement in life, known as "character." Psychologist David Keirsey, in his book *Please Understand Me II*, explains this innate temperament each person has, believer and unbeliever alike, as part of God's workmanship, this way,

> Temperament is a configuration of inclinations, while character is a configuration of habits. . . . Thus, for example, foxes are predisposed—born—to raid hen houses, beavers, to dam up streams, dolphins to affiliate in close-knit schools, and owls to hunt alone in the dark. Each type of creature, unless arrested in its maturation by an unfavorable environment, develops the habit appropriate to its temperament, stealing chickens, building dams, nurturing companions, or hunting at night.[2]

Keirsey argues what is true about animals is true of humans as well. In his book *Mindsight*, Daniel Siegel echoes this thought of Keirsey by noting that

---

2. Kiersey, *Please Understand Me II*, 36.

temperament is determined, for the most part, by one's genetic makeup and not so much influenced by experiences in life.[3] Understood biblically and theologically, each person is designed and gifted as part of God's first article workmanship with certain traits that explain why they do what they do to some degree.

The part of one's personality that is not hardwired is one's character. Keirsey further explains the distinction between the part of one's personality understood as temperament and that which is understood as character in the following way:

> Put another way, our brain is a sort of computer which has temperament for its hardware and character for its software.... Thus temperament is the inborn form of human nature; character, the emergent form, which develops through the interaction of temperament and environment.[4]

A person's character is shaped by many factors, including one's actions, family of origin, societal factors, experience in a church, and faith in God. Christopher Peterson and Martin Seligman, in their book *Character Strengths and Virtues*, note that character is those individual differences in each person that one's environment can shape and, as a result, can change.[5] In his book *A Case for Character*, Joel Biermann defines character as follows: "Character describes the matrix of personal traits that define, direct and name an individual."[6] Character, from which a person also derives a sense of identity, can be considered a gift from God as it also can be shaped by a believer's faith through the working of the Holy Spirit. Awareness of a believer's temperament and character is vital in better discerning their unique identity and how that plays out in their various callings in life in love and service to neighbor.

Temperament—Myers Briggs Assessment

The Myers-Briggs Type Indicator (MBTI) is a well-known and widely used assessment tool developed by the mother-daughter team of Katharine Cook Briggs and Isabela Myers, building off the theory of psychological type

---

3. Siegel, *Mindsight*, 41.
4. Kiersey, *Please Understand Me II*, 36–37.
5. Peterson and Seligman, *Character Strengths and Virtues*, 10.
6. Biermann, *Case for Character*, 13.

formulated by Carl Jung.[7] The MBTI is an assessment tool designed to help bring a deeper awareness of human behavioral complexity and enhance human relationships. In the *MBTI Step II Manual*, Naomi Quenk, Allen Hammer, and Mark Majors explain the underlying theory of psychological type when they write, "A basic tenet of type theory holds that much seemingly random behavior is actually the result of differences in how we perceive the world, how we make sense of our perceptions, where we choose to direct our energy, and how we choose to live in the world."[8] This all has an influence on how a believer engages in living out their vocations in life and how they will serve their neighbors.

The MBTI assessment measures an individual's preferences according to four dichotomies: Extraversion-Introversion (E-I), Sensing-Intuition (S-N), Thinking-Feeling (T-F), and Judging-Perceiving (J-P). The Meyers-Briggs assessment's basic assumption is that each person is born with an innate disposition to develop a preference for one pole or the other of these four dichotomies. As indicated in the *MBTI Manual*, written by Isabel Briggs Myers and other researchers, the recorded preferences to each of these four dichotomies in the assessment yields sixteen possible combinations, known as psychological types.[9] Each of these MBTI types has unique characteristics that have personal implications for better understanding one's personality and impact in interacting with others from working on teams, working in organizations, finding the right career, and implications for college. Here is just one brief overview of each of the sixteen Myers-Briggs types from the *MBTI Manual*.

For this Called2B vocational coaching framework, I will be utilizing the MBTI Step II assessment. Besides measuring each of the four dichotomies' preferences, this assessment tool breaks each dichotomy down to reveal how individuals responded to five different facets within each dichotomy.[10] This exploration helps explain why some individuals have only a slight preference while others have a very strong preference in each of the four dichotomies. An explanation of the MBTI Step II will be given to each participant in this vocational coaching framework before they receive their results. Once that review has taken place, coaching will begin on this assessment tool to help them deepen their awareness of the gift of their personality.

7. Quenk et al., *MBTI Step II Manual*, xi.
8. Quenk et al., *MBTI Step II Manual*, 4.
9. Myers et al., *MBTI Manual*, 7.
10. Quenk et al., *MBTI Step II Manual*, 12.

Setting Up the Coaching Project

Table 1. Sixteen MBTI Types

ISTJ	ISFJ	INFJ	INTJ
I—Depth of concentration	I—Depth of concentration	I—Depth of concentration	I—Depth of concentration
S—Reliance on facts	S—Reliance on facts	N—Grasp of possibilities	N—Grasp of possibilities
T—Logic and analysis	F—Warmth and sympathy	F—Warmth and sympathy	T—Logic and analysis
J—Organization	J—Organization	J—Organization	J—Organization
ISTP	ISFP	INFP	INTP
I—Depth of concentration	I—Depth of concentration	I—Depth of concentration	I—Depth of concentration
S—Reliance on facts	S—Reliance on facts	N—Grasp of possibilities	N—Grasp of possibilities
T—Logic and analysis	F—Warmth and sympathy	F—Warmth and sympathy	T—Logic and analysis
P—Adaptability	P—Adaptability	P—Adaptability	P—Adaptability
ESTP	ESFP	ENFP	ENTP
E—Breadth of interests	E—Breadth of interests	E—Breadth of interests	E—Breadth of interests
S—Reliance on facts	S—Reliance on facts	N—Grasp of possibilities	N—Grasp of possibilities
T—Logic and analysis	F—Warmth and sympathy	F—Warmth and sympathy	T—Logic and analysis
P—Adaptability	P—Adaptability	P—Adaptability	P—Adaptability
ESTJ	ESFJ	ENFJ	ENTJ
E—Breadth of interests	E—Breadth of interests	E—Breadth of interests	E—Breadth of interests
S—Reliance on facts	S—Reliance on facts	N—Grasp of possibilities	N—Grasp of possibilities
T—Logic and analysis	F—Warmth and sympathy	F—Warmth and sympathy	T—Logic and analysis
J—Organization	J—Organization	J—Organization	J—Organization

The following are some potential coaching questions to explore with participants around the MBTI Step II assessment:

1. What things do you do well? What things don't you do well?
2. How do you reenergize yourself after a long day?

3. How do you approach your relationships with others?
4. How do you prefer to take in information?
5. What is your process for making decisions with the information you take in?
6. What approach do you take in orienting yourself to the outer world?
7. How well does the description of your MBTI type describe you? (Descriptions taken from "Introduction to Type.")
8. What aspects of the description resonate with who you are in regards to your personality?
9. What aspects of the description don't resonate with you?
10. Based on your personality type, how do you better understand God's gifting and design in your life?
11. What impact does this increased awareness have on your life?
12. Based on your MBTI type, what are your natural ways of thinking, feeling, and behaving when it comes to your interactions with others?
13. What pitfalls do you need to be aware of based on your MBTI type?
14. What situations in life would be ideal for you? What situations would not be ideal?
15. What are your potential growth areas when it comes to your MBTI type? What are your strengths?
16. What would it look like for you to live life more aligned to your personality type in your love and service to others?

Character and Virtue—VIA Assessment

The VIA assessment is an additional coaching tool, to be utilized in this vocational coaching framework, to help participants grow in their awareness regarding their character. Growing out of the research of the new field of positive psychology, Christopher Peterson and Martin Seligman led a team of fifty-five researchers to answer the question "what does good character mean, and how it can be measured?"[11] Their research across various cultures and religious traditions over history identified what they termed

---

11. Peterson and Seligman, *Primer in Positive Psychology*, 138.

Setting Up the Coaching Project

"twenty-four character strengths" that were, in their view, universally valued.[12] Peterson and Seligman view these character strengths as the psychological way in which virtue is lived out and displayed.[13]

During their research, they also identified six core virtues, across cultural and religious traditions, under which these twenty-four character strengths were organized.[14] Four of these six core virtues, identified in VIA's taxonomy, are the four virtues of courage, justice, temperance, and wisdom, as taught by Aristotle (a.k.a. the "cardinal virtues").[15] Thomas Aquinas's three "theological virtues" of faith, hope, and charity (love), as identified from St. Paul in 1 Cor 13:13, are not named specifically among VIA's six virtues. However, in the view of Peterson and Seligman, faith and hope are represented within the virtue of "transcendence," and charity (love), within the virtue of "humanity."[16] Hope and love are also explicitly listed as two of the twenty-four VIA character strengths. Here are VIA's classifications of their twenty-four character strengths and six virtues:

Table 2. Twenty-Four VIA Character Strengths

WISDOM	COURAGE	HUMANITY	JUSTICE	TEMPERANCE	TRANSCENDENCE
Creativity	Bravery	Love	Teamwork	Forgiveness	Appreciation of Beauty and Excellence
Curiosity	Perseverance	Kindness	Fairness	Humility	Gratitude
Judgement	Honesty	Social Intelligence	Leadership	Prudence	Hope
Love of Learning	Zest			Self-Regulation	Humor
Perspective					Spirituality

For this vocational coaching framework, I will be using Joel Biermann's definition of character as previously referenced before. He additionally defines virtue in the following way: "Virtues are the specific traits, skills, and behaviors that serve both to define and guide those on the journey toward

---

12. Peterson and Seligman, *Primer in Positive Psychology*, 138–45.
13. Peterson and Seligman, *Character Strengths and Virtues*, 13.
14. Peterson and Seligman, *Character Strengths and Virtues*, 33–40.
15. Peterson and Seligman, *Character Strengths and Virtues*, 46–47.
16. Peterson and Seligman, *Character Strengths and Virtues*, 47.

the agreed-upon *telos* [goal]."[17] As one lives a virtuous life aimed at some goal of living or becoming, one's character is shaped and formed, for good or for bad. So, what is the goal, or telos, believers should aim for in living a virtuous life? That goal, according to Biermann, is to live the life that humanity was originally created and now redeemed to live in Christ, given shape by the Ten Commandments.[18] As Biermann states, "Simply put, human destiny, our telos, is to be all that God designed and created us to be—in other words, to be fully human."[19] As the second Adam, Jesus came not just to save humanity for eternity but that believers may also bear his image as the heavenly man (1 Cor 15:45–49). Ultimately, the telos for believers is to grow in Christ-likeness as they seek to love and serve their neighbors in their various horizontal callings in life.[20]

How does one grow in Christ-likeness to live more aligned with who God has created and now redeemed each believer to be? Dallas Willard, in his book *Renovation of the Heart*, proposes a model for spiritual transformation that is useful in coaching for growth in virtue and character development called "VIM."[21] VIM stands for "Vision, Intention, Means." The vision, or telos, for believers, in this life, is to grow in Christ-likeness, to be more fully human. This telos is not in terms of a believer's vertical relationship with God, for by grace through faith one is already in Christ and, as previously noted, their ultimate identity is secured as a free gift from God. A believer's telos, instead, is to grow in Christ-likeness as one lives out their ultimate identity in Jesus through their unique identity in love and service to their neighbors, horizontally. The means that have been given by God to do so are the Word and Sacraments through which the Holy Spirit works to produce the fruit of the Spirit (Gal 5:22–23) and a believer experiences growth in the kingdom virtues of faith, hope, and love (1 Cor 13:13). There are also spiritual disciplines and the Ten Commandments that can be used as means to mold and shape a believer's character. The key to this transformation of one's character is the intentional use of both the Means of Grace, through which the Spirit works, and other spiritual practices towards growth in character—a cooperation with God in one's life of sanctification.

---

17. Biermann, *Case for Character*, 12.
18. Biermann, *Case for Character*, 78.
19. Biermann, *Case for Character*, 144.
20. Biermann, *Case for Character*, 129.
21. Willard, *Renovation of the Heart*, 85.

In regards to the intentional use of spiritual disciplines and habits to shape character, Biermann discusses the importance of what is called "habituation" when he writes, "Habituation is the practice of virtuous acts and the cultivation of pious habits."[22] As a believer lives virtuously in love and service to their neighbor, an imprint is left on an individual's character.[23] One act of virtue alone does not transform a person's character. However, repeated virtuous acts can. In his book *Brain Savvy Leaders*, Charles Stone notes how the field of neuroscience has demonstrated that what one pays attention to creates new neural pathways within the brain, for, according to Hebb's law, neurons that "fire together wire together."[24] It is because of these new synaptic linkages, created by experiences in life, that one grows and learns.[25] From this rewiring of the brain, new habits and behaviors of being are formed. This neuroplasticity shows that virtuous acts lead to the right thinking as much as, perhaps even more than, right thinking leads to doing virtuous acts, in terms of character development and spiritual formation.

Another helpful tool for coaching believers in regards to their character and living a virtuous life comes from N. T. Wright, in his book *After You Believe*. Wright echoes Biermann in laying out a biblical and theological case that after their salvation, a believer's telos, or goal, is to be restored in Christ, to be truly human.[26] He states, "The Christian vision of virtue is the vision of the pathway towards this goal."[27] Wright explains how, through Jesus, a believer's original vocation of being God's royal priesthood—those created by God to rule and serve over creation on his behalf—has now been restored in one's identity in Christ.[28] This created and now redeemed identity of being the royal priesthood is also the believer's future identity in the new creation, which they are to learn to practice in their lives today through a virtuous life.[29]

To learn to live out this created and now redeemed identity freely given to believers through faith in Jesus, Wright presents his "virtuous circle,"

---

22. Biermann, *Case for Character*, 93.
23. Biermann, *Case for Character*, 94.
24. Stone, *Brain Savvy Leaders*, 24.
25. Siegel, *Mindsight*, 40.
26. Wright, *After You Believe*, 74–75.
27. Wright, *After You Believe*, 74–75.
28. Wright, *After You Believe*, 80–81.
29. Wright, *After You Believe*, 82–83.

which contains practices and activities through which those in Christ can experience transformation in their minds to the point where these virtuous practices become like second nature to them.[30] The five practices of Wright's virtuous circle are (1) Scripture, (2) Stories, (3) Examples, (4) Community, and (5) Practices.[31] It is this practice of virtuous acts with the goal, or telos, of living out one's identity in Christ that begins to shape a believer's character. This can be a helpful coaching tool when paired with Willard's VIM model, especially in the exploration of those means through which the vision of growing in Christ-likeness takes place.

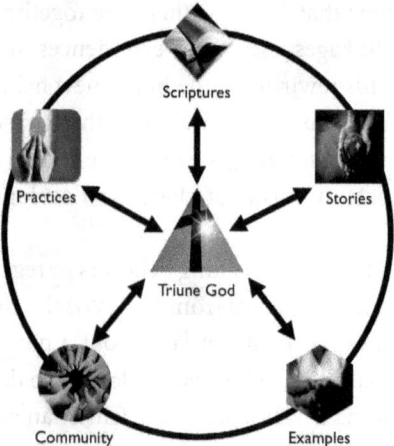

Figure 4. The Virtuous Circle

The following are some potential coaching questions to explore with participants around the VIA assessment:

1. How accurately do your VIA results reflect the essence of who you are at your core?
2. Which VIA character strengths have people recognized in you in the past?
3. What do you sense are those things that you value as a result of your VIA character strengths? What things motivate you?
4. How do you see yourself living out your VIA character strengths in your life currently? (personal, family, career, church, community, etc.)

30. Wright, *After You Believe*, 259–60.
31. Wright, *After You Believe*, 261–82.

5. How are you under-using or overusing your VIA character strengths in your life right now?
6. What would it look like if you were living a life more aligned with your VIA character strengths?
7. How can you live out your VIA character strengths more intentionally in your life and faith walk?
8. What are some of the character qualities and virtues of Jesus that you would want more of in your life?
9. What are some of the means God has made available to you to grow in Christ-likeness? (Share the virtuous circle.)
10. Where does Jesus need to do some work in your character to better reflect his identity in you?
11. What is the part that Jesus plays in shaping your character and what part do you play?
12. How can you love and serve your neighbors in a way that aligns with and harnesses your VIA character strengths?
13. What is keeping you from doing so right now and how can you overcome it?
14. If you were to develop and harness one of your top VIA character strengths, in your life, over the next three months, which one would you want to focus on?
15. If you were to develop one of your lesser VIA character strengths, in your life, in the next three months, which one would you want to focus on?
16. Where do you need encouragement and support in living out your VIA character strengths?

Passions in Life

The second aspect of a believer's Divine GPS to be explored is the gift of one's passions in life. On the surface this may seem a strange thing to explore for Christians since there is so much in the Scriptures about not pursuing ungodly passions. In Titus 2:11–12 (ESV), we hear, "For the grace of God has appeared, bringing salvation for all people, training us to renounce ungodliness and worldly passions, and to live self-controlled, upright, and godly lives in the present age." Also, in 1 Pet 2:11 (ESV), we are encouraged, "Beloved, I urge you as sojourners and exiles to abstain from the passions of the flesh, which wage war against your soul." At first glance, it would appear that pursuing one's passions is not a God-pleasing thing for believers to do.

However, it is crucial to understand what passions truly are to appreciate the value for exploring them in a believer's life as they seek to live out their calling in Christ in love and service to their neighbors. Collins, in his book on Christian coaching, defines passion in the following way: "Passion is a powerful underlying emotion that energizes and drives us."[32] As such, passions serve as the gas in one's tank to energize them in life. In her book *Thriveorship*, Gabrielle Hamen-Kieffer, an organizational coach, explains passion in the following way: "Passion is energy fueled by powerful emotions or appetites such as love, joy, hatred, anger, or greed. It moves you in powerful ways."[33] Passion, at its core and essence, is love for something, either directed towards those things that are honorable in this world and to God or bad. That direction to which one's passions is aimed will be determined largely by their character. It is the tension between the reign of God and the reign of Satan within a believer's heart that directs how one's passions are lived out. Also, there is a battle between the new man and the old man, as described by Paul in Rom 7:7–8:4.

When Jesus turned over the tables of the money changers in the temple in John 2:13–17, we hear how the disciples remembered the words of Ps 69:9 (ESV), "Zeal for your house has consumed me." The Greek word for the "zeal" Jesus displayed is ζῆλος, meaning "to have a deep concern for or devotion to someone or something."[34] Jesus was filled with love, with concern, with passion, for his father's house and it moved him to do something about the abuse that he witnessed. That is passion. Also, it is worthy to note that Jesus' suffering and death upon the cross is widely known as "the passion." What would move the Father to send Jesus to be the final perfect sacrifice for this fallen and broken world that we see on that Good Friday long ago? In short, it is his deep love and passion for the human race (John 3:16–17). Passion can also be seen as lived out by the great heroes of the faith: Moses in his passion to see his people freed from the hand of Pharaoh, David in his passion to build a house for the LORD, Solomon in

---

32. Collins, *Christian Coaching*, 150.
33. Hamen-Kieffer, *Thriveorship*, 127.
34. Louw and Nida, *Greek-English Lexicon*, 293.

his pursuit of wisdom, and Paul in not only his desire to see salvation come to his own people but also to bring the gospel to the gentiles.

In this vocational coaching framework, participants will explore how their passions, those God-pleasing things they love and have an interest in and/or the deep concerns that move their heart, can be harnessed as they seek to discover and live out their calling in Christ in their horizontal callings in life. Hamen-Kieffer explains, "Your passions are the flame that warm and ignite your talents, values, and, most importantly, your purpose."[35] One's passions can fuel a person in living out their vocations, especially when things get difficult in life. Passions can also unite people together in common service. In a newly released Barna Report entitled *Better Together*, produced in partnership with Lutheran Hour Ministries, found that "62 percent of practicing Christians who participated in a community group shared a strong passion for the cause with their fellow group members."[36] It would seem that serving together around a mutual passion leads to deeper engagement and positive outcomes.[37]

Veith encourages those seeking to find clarity in one's vocations also to explore their God-given interests. He does so by stating, "'What do you want to be?' is indeed a good question. But what you are is in many ways given. Even your wants—your desires, your dreams, your choices—are a unique function of who you are."[38] In many ways, one's interests, one's loves, one's passions, when aligned with God's good and pleasing will, are a part of his divine gifting in a believer's life, and, as such, worthy of exploration. Benne encourages this vocational exploration of passion when he states, "Clarity about oneself includes an honest appraisal of skills, talents, practical and moral strengths, and what gives mature satisfaction, as well as an assessment of how one best serves. One tries to identify one's deep-running interests, not one's surface inclinations."[39] In the end, to ignore God-ordained passions can feel like something that runs counter not only to one's heart but to the very will of God as well.[40] To help believers better discern their passions in life I have designed the following passion assessment:

35. Hamen-Kieffer, *Thriveorship*, 127.
36. Barna Group, *Better Together*, 43.
37. Barna Group, *Better Together*, 43.
38. Veith, *God at Work*, 52.
39. Benne, *Ordinary Saints*, 173.
40. Collins, *Christian Coaching*, 152.

Who Have You Been Called to Be?

Table 3. Called2B Passion Assessment

People Passion—What people do I have a heart for? (Limit answers to 3–5)

Abuse Victims	Divorced	Men	Parents	Street Kids
Adults	Empty Nesters	Middle Schoolers	Parents of Teens	Teen Moms
Business Professionals	Engaged Couples	Minority Communities	Prisoners	Teens
Career Women	Grieving	The Poor	Seekers	Unemployed
Children	Homeless	New Believers	Seniors	Visitors to Church
College Students	Hospitalized	New Church Members	Single Parents	Widows and Widowers
Couples	Infants	New Parents	Singles	Women
Disabled	Immigrants	Newlyweds	Gen Z	Millennials
Veterans	Refugees	Shut Ins	Orphans	Other

Issue Passion—What issue(s) or concern(s) do I feel most strongly about? (Limit answers to 3–5)

Abortion Awareness	Discipleship	Marriage Issues	Housing	Racism
Addictions	Divorce Care	Ministry Involvement	Human Rights	Reaching the Lost
Administration	Economics	Overseas/Domestic Missions	Hunger	Social Issues
AIDS	Education	Parenting	Injustice	Technology
The Arts	The Environment	Politics	International Issues	Teen Concerns
Child Care	Family Issues	Poverty	Interpersonal Relations	Terminal Illness
Counseling	Financial Issues	Disaster Relief	Legal Issues	Violence
Creative Projects	Health Care	Prisons	Literacy	Worship
Defending the Faith	Sexual Identity Issues/LGBTQ+	Community Development	Immigration	Other

Setting Up the Coaching Project

Interest Passion—What interest(s) excite you the most?
(Limit answers to 3–5)

Movies/Film Making	Music	Books	Science	Sports
Outdoors	Business	Fashion	Medical Field	Personal Health/ Fitness
Personal Development	Drawing/ Painting	Teaching	Faith/Religion	Woodworking
Writing	Engineering	Hospitality	Sightseeing/ Travel	Cooking/ Baking
Wine/Beer	Entrepreneurship	Playing Games	Knitting/ Sewing	Hiking/ Camping
Biking	Walking/ Running	Dining Out	Collecting	Theatre/Acting
Shopping	Interior Design	Architecture	Mentoring/Life Coaching	Psychology
Social Media	Graphic Design	Web Development	Sports Coaching	Public Service
Leadership/ Management	Organizational Development	Gardening/ Farming	Coffee/Tea	Other

The following are some potential coaching questions to explore areas of passion with participants:

1. What things get you excited about waking up in the morning?
2. What topics could keep you up all night talking?
3. What things captured your imagination as a child? How do those things still capture your imagination?
4. What life experiences give you the most enjoyment, fulfillment, or satisfaction?
5. What activities do you enjoy doing in which you seem to lose yourself and all track of time?
6. If I asked those close to you to describe what energizes you, how would they respond?
7. What issues, ministries, or possible needs excite or concern you the most?
8. If you had unlimited resources and knew that you couldn't fail, what would you do for the kingdom of God and the world?

Who Have You Been Called to Be?

9. Answer the following statement, "When I _____, I feel God's pleasure."

10. From these questions, what do you sense are those things that you are truly passionate about in life?

11. From the Called2B Passion Assessment, what people, issues or interests are you most passionate about? Which two or three ignite your heart the most?

12. How are you currently living out those passions in your life and faith walk?

13. What things is Jesus truly passionate about?

14. What would it look like to live out your passions, in alignment to those things that Jesus is passionate about, in love and service to others?

15. How would life be different if you were able to live life aligned to your passions? How would you be different?

16. What is keeping you from living a life of passion right now? How could you overcome it?

Living Your Strengths

The third aspect of a believer's Divine GPS to be explored in this vocational coaching framework is one's God-given talents. The CliftonStrengths®[41] assessment (a.k.a. StrengthsFinder) aids people in identifying their innate talents, their naturally recurring patterns of thought, feelings, and behaviors that can be productively applied in life.[42] There are thirty-four different talent themes (unique combinations of talents) that the assessment measures that have been found can lead to success in life.[43] With the addition of knowledge, skills, and experience, one can develop their talents into building a strengths-based life.[44] The following are the thirty-four talent themes

---

41. Gallup®, CliftonStrengths® and the CliftonStrengths 34 Themes of Talent are trademarks of Gallup, Inc. All rights reserved.
   42. Buckingham and Clifton, *Now, Discover Your Strengths*, 48.
   43. Buckingham and Clifton, *Now, Discover Your Strengths*, 12
   44. Buckingham and Clifton, *Now, Discover Your Strengths*, 29

assessed for in the CliftonStrengths® assessment, organized into their four domains, presented by Tom Rath in his book *Strengths Based Leadership*:[45]

Table 4. CliftonStrengths Four Domains

Executing	Influencing	Relationship Building	Strategic Thinking
Achiever®	Activator®	Adaptability®	Analytical®
Arranger®	Command®	Developer®	Context®
Belief®	Communication®	Connectedness®	Futuristic®
Consistency®	Competition®	Empathy®	Ideation®
Deliberative®	Maximizer®	Harmony®	Input®
Discipline®	Self-Assurance®	Includer®	Intellection®
Focus®	Significance®	Individualization®	Learner®
Responsibility®	Woo®	Positivity®	Strategic®
Restorative™		Relator®	

Understood in terms of Luther's teaching on vocation, these talents are given as part of God's workmanship and design, as Paul describes in Eph 2:10, to use for good works in love and service to one's neighbors in the horizontal areas of responsibility in life. Veith describes how the believer's talents can be used through their vocations in life to bless one's neighbor when he writes,

> In God's design, each person is to love his or her neighbors and to serve them with the gifts appropriated to each vocation. This means that I serve you with my talents, and you serve me with your talents. The result is a divine division of labor in which everyone is constantly giving and receiving in a vast interchange, a unity of diverse people in a social order whose substance and energy is love.[46]

To service one another with the talents God has provided is part of God's economy in how he uses each person to bless others, uniquely, in and through their stations in life. Luther also encourages the use of a believer's talents, like tools, to accomplish the calling he or she has received when he explains, in his commentary on Genesis,

> This is true in all other actions of our common life. I must not cut the tree down with my nose, but I must take an ax or a saw.

---

45. Rath and Conchie, *Strengths Based Leadership*, 24–26.
46. Veith, *God at Work*, 40.

> The tree must not be cut down with a blade of straw, but with an ax. And this is why God has given man reason, perception, and strength. Use these as means and gifts of God.[47]

As such, each believer should utilize those things that have been gifted to them as part of God's workmanship and design in love and service to others.

In a powerful statement that highlights a fundamental understanding of the relationship between talents and vocation, that one can only be who God has created and called them to be, Tom Rath, in his book *StrengthsFinder 2.0*, makes the following observation:

> You can be anything you want to be, if you just try hard enough. . . . This might sound like a heretical point of view, especially for those of us who grew up believing the essential American myth that we could become anything we wanted. Yet it's clear from Gallup's research that each person has greater potential for success in specific areas, and the key to human development is building on who you already are.[48]

Albert Winesman, in his book *Living Your Strengths*, applies a faith perspective on this idea, shared by Rath, of helping people begin to discern how their God-given talents can be lived out in a believer's daily life when he explains, "It gives us permission to stop trying to be who we are not and concentrate on who we are—who we were originally created to be."[49] We can't be whatever we dream we can be; life is not a Disney movie. However, we can be who God has created and redeemed us to be. The CliftonStrengths® assessment is a powerful tool that can help believers with that discernment process.

In two different kingdom parables of the fig tree in Matt 21:18–19 and Luke 13:6–9, we hear from Jesus about God's desire for believers to produce fruit in their lives. Helping believers bear fruit for the kingdom through their various callings in life, ultimately, comes down to a matter of stewardship. Miller and Hall discuss how coaching can help believers grow in the stewardship of their God-given gifts and talents when they write,

> Coaching supports Christian stewardship by giving positive attention to the results of a life lived with intention. Coaching conversations often begin by acknowledging that bad or little fruit is being

---

47. Pelikan et al., *Luther's Works*, vol. 8, 95.
48. Rath, *StrengthsFinder 2.0*, 7–8.
49. Winesman et al., *Living Your Strengths*, 11.

produced. People are not satisfied with the results they are getting and want better results."[50]

A study conducted by Gallup® revealed that more than half of believers (53 percent) do not strongly agree with the statement "In my congregation, I regularly have the opportunity to do what I do best."[51] Unfortunately, many believers are asked to serve in roles in their congregations without any investment in helping them discover their gifts and strengths.[52] Creswell ponders a solution to this problem when she asks, "What if the structure, the programs, the ministries of the church were organized in a way to maximize the gifts, talents, skills, personalities—*strengths*—of both ministers and laypeople so that all were united in a common God-given vision?"[53] Coaching around the CliftonStrengths® assessment can be a powerful approach to empower believers to steward their God-given gifts and talents more effectively in their churches, as well as in living out their calling in Christ in their other areas of responsibility in life.

The following are some potential coaching questions to explore areas of strengths with participants:

1. As you review your CliftonStrengths® results, how well does it describe you?[54]
2. Of all the things you do well in life, what are one or two things that you do especially well? What correlation do you see with your CliftonStrengths® talents?
3. Which parts of your current calling(s) in life do you enjoy the most and why?
4. From your top five, what talents do you use in your current calling(s)? How do they help you live out these areas of responsibility?
5. What is a highlight that we can celebrate in your various callings? How do you see your talents in action in those callings?
6. As you consider your daily frustrations in life, how do your talents help you not only understand but navigate these frustrations better?

50. Miller and Hall, *Coaching for Christian Leaders*, 14–15.
51. Winesman et al., *Living Your Strengths*, 1.
52. Creswell, *Coaching for Excellence*, 250.
53. Creswell, *Coaching for Excellence*, 5.
54. Gallup®, CliftonStrengths® and the CliftonStrengths 34 Themes of Talent are trademarks of Gallup, Inc. All rights reserved.

7. Where do you see your talents at work in your relationships in life? With family? With friends? With coworkers? With your manager/boss? Within your church? With your community?
8. How can you intentionally aim your talents to better love and serve your neighbors in your various areas of responsibilities in life?
9. If we have been created on purpose for a purpose, how might God desire to work through your talents so that you can be a greater blessing to others in your various callings in life?
10. Based on your top talents, what do you see as your role within the body of Christ?
11. Who can you partner with who has complementary talents to your own?
12. Of your top five talents, which one or two would you want to develop first into a greater strength in your life?
13. What is one measurable goal that you can create to which you can apply your talents in order to see greater progress and performance in the next week, three months, one year?
14. What do you want to commit to as a result of this coaching conversation?
15. How are you different as a result of this coaching conversation?
16. What encouragement and support do you need as you seek to, more intentionally, harness your top five talents in order to build a Strengths-based life?

Coaching for Empowerment—Heart, Soul, Mind, and Strength

The second element in this Called2B vocational coaching framework is Empowerment—connecting believers to Jesus in heart, soul, mind, and strength. In the field of coaching there is a growing focus on the topic of well-being. In a whitepaper published in 2014 called "An Introduction to Wellness Coaching," Dr. Jeffry Auerbach notes that wellness coaching is a booming field, especially among three specific populations: (1) Fully healthy individuals who want to further increase their quality of their life and relationships; (2) Moderately well individuals who have specific health, well-being, and social goals; and (3) Individuals who have a chronic or acute illness who want specific support, guidance, and assistance related to enhancing the quality of their life.⁵⁵ This type of wellness coaching focuses on everything from stress reduction, addressing health concerns, establishing wellness goals, integrating information about health and wellness into healthy behaviors, improving long-term motivation and follow-through on many health goals, time management, etc.⁵⁶ Well-being and flourishing are also the major focus in the field of positive psychology, which, as mentioned in chapter 3, is a foundational school of thought for coaching.⁵⁷

How should believers understand this concept of well-being biblically and theologically? In John 10:10 (ESV), Jesus declares, "The thief comes only to steal and kill and destroy. I came that they may have life and have it abundantly." This abundant life that Jesus says that he has come to bring to believers first and foremost is concerned with knowing God's saving love by grace through faith in one's vertical relationship with God. However, is there something more that God is calling believers to experience in this life once they come to know Jesus' saving love? Is life abundant only about eternity, or is life abundant in Jesus also a present reality that can be experienced and lived out horizontally in all of one's callings in life? Granted, life is lived in a fallen and broken world, filled with sin internally and externally. However, the life Jesus came to deliver for believers is to be "so abundant (περισσός) as to be considered more than what one would expect or anticipate."⁵⁸ Ultimately, the question to be answered is: if so, what does it look like for believers to thrive and flourish both in their relationship with God as well as their relationship with their neighbors in this life?

In Luke 10:25–28, Jesus has an encounter with an expert of the law who asks him, "Teacher, what must I do to inherit eternal life?" In typical fashion, Jesus responds to this inquiry not with an answer but with a question of his own. He asks this expert, "What is written in the Law? How do you read it?" To this question, the expert of the law responds, "Love the Lord your God with all of your heart and with all of your soul and with all of your strength and with all of your mind; and love your neighbor as yourself." Jesus responds to this summation of the Ten Commandments, which governs both one's vertical relationship with God (commandments one to three) as well as one's horizontal relationship with one's neighbor (commandments four to ten), in the affirmative, "Do this and you will live."

55. Auerbach, *Introduction to Wellness Coaching*, 1.
56. Auerbach, *Introduction to Wellness Coaching*, 2.
57. Seligman, *Flourish*, 13.
58. Louw and Nida, *Greek-English Lexicon*, 598–99. Based on the semantic domains.

Who Have You Been Called to Be?

There were still some heart issues for Jesus to discuss with this expert of the law since he was seeking to justify himself by his doing rather than seeking to be justified in his being in Christ. However, God's entire purpose and will for humanity and, with it, human-flourishing is expressed in these words. Yet, the connecting point between these two callings to love God and to love neighbor is the believer's calling of the four aspects of self that Jesus refers to in this passage—heart, soul, mind, and strength.

It is important to note that what empowers believers to even begin to love God and love others as they love themselves is that they must be made alive in God's love in Christ. John states in his first epistle, "In this is love, not that we have loved God but that he loved us and sent his Son to be the propitiation for our sins" (1 John 4:10 ESV). As believers experience Jesus' love, they are empowered to begin to love God in their vertical calling with him and to begin to love their neighbors in their horizontal callings in life in a way that pleases God and engages their whole self. Believers are called to love God with their whole heart (καρδία), which was understood biblically as the source of a person's psychological life, including heart, inner self, and mind, which was also thought of in terms of liver, stomach, or bowels.[59] They are to love God with their whole soul (ψυχή), which was associated with the essence of life in terms of thinking, willing, feeling, and the essence of their being, including purpose or desire involved in faith.[60] They are to love God with their whole strength (ἰσχύς), which was associated with personal potential involving capacity and strength.[61] A derivative of this Greek word for strength (ἰσχύω) also refers to the quality of physical strength involving the body.[62] And lastly, but not least, they are to love God with their whole mind (διάνοια), which was associated with the content of their thinking and reasoning.[63]

It would appear from these biblical definitions of heart, soul, mind, and strength that it is almost impossible to distinguish between these four different aspects of self fully. Correctly understood, Jesus is saying that believers are to love God and others with the whole of our being. This understanding would not be so far from the truth when one considers recent research related to neuroscience as it pertains to spirituality. There is such

---

59. Louw and Nida, *Greek-English Lexicon*, 320.
60. Louw and Nida, *Greek-English Lexicon*, 320.
61. Louw and Nida, *Greek-English Lexicon*, 675.
62. Louw and Nida, *Greek-English Lexicon*, 699.
63. Louw and Nida, *Greek-English Lexicon*, 350–51.

an interconnection between these different aspects of one's life that while they are distinct, they are also an interrelated whole. Stone describes this interconnection when he writes,

> We have both a body and a soul mysteriously unified. What goes on in our souls affects our bodies and brains. What we pay attention to can actually change our brain's neuropathways—their plasticity. If you regularly read, study, and apply God's word, you will create connections in your brain that reinforce a biblical worldview. Likewise, our body influences our soul. For example, the next time you don't sleep well, you'll find it more difficult to pay attention to God's quiet voice in your devotional time the next day. Sleepy bodies affect our minds and, hence, our effectiveness.[64]

The unique quality of each person's existence is as a hybrid spiritual/physical being of God's creation. Unfortunately, there is a dualistic tendency within Christianity that separates concern for the soul from concern for the rest of a person. For example, what happens in the church is seen as holy, while what happens in the rest of life is seen as secular. The same is true for people. A holistic approach to discipleship takes seriously each of these four aspects of self (heart, soul, mind, and strength) while recognizing the interconnectedness of these aspects in their entirety. Jesus redeemed not just a believer's soul but the whole as part of his fallen, yet still very good, creation.

This second element of Empowerment is a piece that I felt like I hadn't fully developed in this vocational coaching framework until reading Scott Eblin's book *Overworked and Overwhelmed*. Eblin writes about coaching in terms of being more mindful, especially in living out what he terms as one's Life GPS. I was especially intrigued by the routines he writes about regarding physical health, mental health, relational health, and spiritual health.[65] Eblin stresses the importance of caring for each of these four aspects of self when he writes, "Effective routines often have a ripple effect that enables you to show up at your best more often by cutting across one or more of these four domains."[66] What allows believers to begin to show up at their best, in terms of their vertical relationship in Christ and their horizontal calling to love and serve their neighbors in life, is to make sure they take time to be empowered in these same four aspects of self—heart, soul, mind, and strength. Ultimately, self-care is not selfish. Dr. Ryan Niemiec, the

---

64. Stone, *Brain Savvy Leaders*, 23.
65. Eblin, *Overworked and Overwhelmed*, 52.
66. Eblin, *Overworked and Overwhelmed*, 54.

director for the VIA Institute on Character Education and president of the International Positive Psychology Association (IPPA), Spirituality/Meaning Division, said during a breakout session as part of the 2021 IPPA "Evidence in Action" online conference, "Taking care of our own well-being is a social act; it has a ripple effect to others."[67]

The approach utilized at this point in this vocational coaching framework model to empower participants regarding their heart, soul, mind, and strength aligns very well with the "Four-Step Human Change Process" described by Bacon and Voss.[68] The first step is "Building Awareness" by establishing a baseline and gathering information through the "4 Aspects of Self Wheel" I developed for this Empowerment step in the coaching process. The self-scoring scale is developed like scoring in golf; the lower the number, the better the score. A score of 10 represents being very far away from alignment with Jesus, and a score of 1 represents being in complete alignment with Jesus in this part of their life. Next, participants are asked what a one- or two-point change in each aspect of their life would look like in growing in their Christ-likeness. Second in this coaching process on Empowerment is "Building Commitment" by creating a sense of urgency. This building of commitment is done by asking what steps the coachee could begin to take to intentionally grow in their Christ-likeness in each aspect of their life.

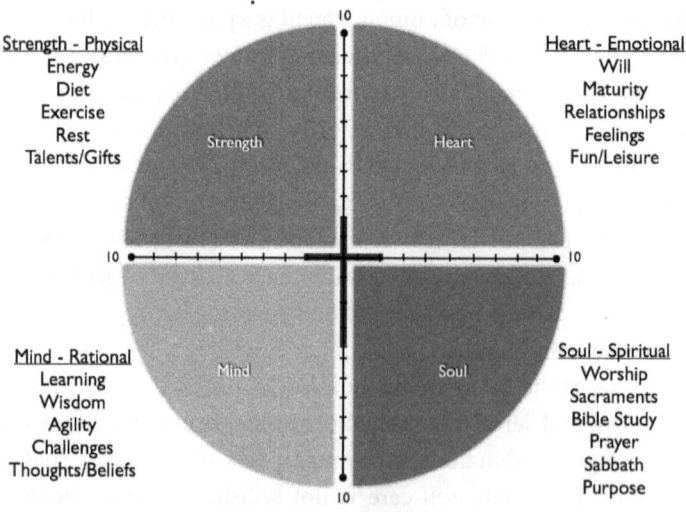

Figure 5. 4 Aspects of Self Wheel

67. Niemiec, "Evidence in Action."
68. Bacon and Voss, *Adaptive Coaching*, 248.

Setting Up the Coaching Project

The third step is to start "Building Practice" by coaching participants to develop an empowerment plan for themselves with this question in mind: "What empowers me?" Participants will create SMART (Specific, Measurable, Attainable, Relevant, Time Bound) goals related to this question regarding their heart, soul, mind, and strength. While there will be specific actions that will be unique to each of these aspects of self, there will likely also be a significant amount of overlap in developing a comprehensive plan. Finally, the last step in the coaching process is "Building Accountability." Here, the coaching provides the support, encouragement, and accountability needed to put these SMART goals into action. The ultimate goal in coaching within this element of Empowerment is to help participants develop rhythms and routines that help them begin to experience, to a greater degree, the abundant life of Christ in their relationship with God and their relationship with their neighbors, in order to be a greater blessing.

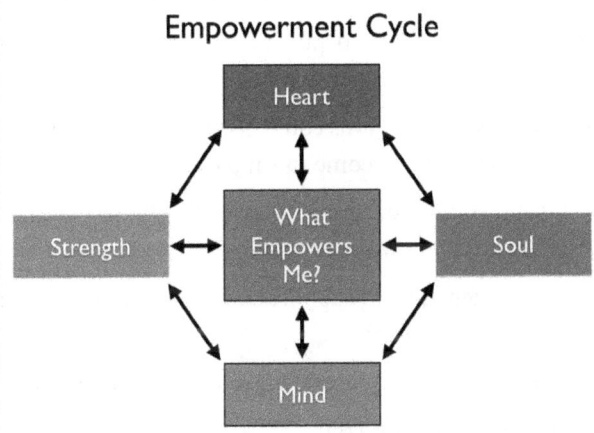

Figure 6. Empowerment Cycle

The following are some potential coaching questions to explore this element of empowering believers in heart, soul, mind and strength:

1. What does it look like when you are fully charged?
2. What things in life drain your batteries?
3. How would you describe your overall well-being currently (heart, soul, mind, and strength)?

4. (Introduce the "4 Aspects of Self Wheel.") On a scale of 10 to 1 (10 being far away from Christ-likeness and 1 being totally aligned with Jesus) how would you rate this area of your life right now?
5. What would a one- or two-point positive change look like in this area of your life?
6. What can you do to effect this change? What do you need to rely on God for?
7. What are one or two small things you could do right now to make the biggest impact in each of these aspects of your life?
8. How could you leverage what is going well in one aspect of your life to help improve another aspect of your life?
9. What is one SMART goal you could create, in regards to each aspect of your life, in order to develop an empowerment plan? (Review SMART goals.)
10. What would it look like to potentially merge any of your SMART goals into a more comprehensive well-being goal?
11. What obstacles or objections could get in your way of achieving these goals? How can you overcome this interference?
12. What resources can you draw upon internally or externally to help you execute this empowerment plan?
13. What encouragement and support do you need as you seek to live out your empowerment plan?
14. How would you like to be accountable for your empowerment plan?
15. How can I be praying for you?

Coaching for Kingdom Impact—Loving One's Neighbors

The third and final element in this Called2B vocational coaching framework is Impact—connecting believers to the world in relevant and transformative ways. This element is a reminder that Jesus hasn't just saved believers for eternity, but he has also redeemed them for his purposes here today. That purpose for which they are saved is to be a conduit of God's common grace, his provision and care for this world, by being a blessing to one's neighbors. Additionally, it is to serve as a conduit of Jesus' saving grace as

Setting Up the Coaching Project

each believer shares the good news of the gospel with those in their life. In this element, coaching participants will explore what it looks like to live out their authentic identity in Christ (both their ultimate identity that comes by grace through faith in Jesus, as well as their unique identity of God's workmanship, gifting, and design) in love and service to their neighbors in their various areas of responsibilities in life. Coachees will explore what this looks like to live out their calling in Christ in each of the four stations of life that Luther discusses in his teaching on vocation—church, family, work (what I will be calling "lifework"), and society.

There are a few foundational scriptural references for this element of Impact in this vocational coaching framework. Besides Luke 10:25–28, in which we hear God's revealed will and purpose for humanity expressed as loving God in one's vertical relationship and loving neighbor in one's horizontal relationships in life, there are also the apostle Paul's words in Rom 13:8–10 (NIV). In this passage of Scripture, Paul encourages his hearers in their horizontal callings in life with others:

> Let no debt remain outstanding, except the continuing debt to love one another, for whoever loves others has fulfilled the law. The commandments, "You shall not commit adultery," "You shall not murder," "You shall not steal," "You shall not covet," and whatever other command there may be, are summed up in this one command: "Love your neighbor as yourself." Love does no harm to a neighbor. Therefore love is the fulfillment of the law.

Like the expert of the law in his encounter with Jesus, Paul boils commandments four through ten down to how one should love and serve their neighbor. For Paul, it's all about love, for love is the fulfillment of the law. As is seen in Luther's teaching on vocation, believers ascend to God by faith and descend in love to serve their neighbors in life. For the believer, instead of asking the question "what does the law demand of me to do?" a better question, from these words of Paul, would be "what would love call me to do for the sake of my neighbor?"

Before exploring how participants will begin to live out their calling in Christ in each of the four areas of responsibility in life, the first step in this vocational coaching framework is to take them through a coaching tool called the "Basic Calling Model." I have done extensive research to determine the origin of this calling model, but to no avail. The Basic Calling Model consists of three circles that intersect. I've adapted this coaching tool to help participants process how their Divine GPS can best be utilized in love and service to their neighbors. The first circle represents what one's gift of personality (both temperament and character) and one's strengths (talents) contribute. The second circle represents what makes their heart sing, which are their passions in life, both their interests and concerns. Lastly, the final circle represents the question "who needs what I have to offer?" The original version of this Basic Calling Model asked instead, "What does the world need?" Asking what the world needs is too large a question and can be rather overwhelming for people. It is better to coach believers to discern who, before them, are their immediate neighbors, whom they can serve each day with their Divine GPS in their various areas of responsibilities in life.

It is at the intersection of these three circles that one begins to discern their "Calling Sweet Spot," their unique vocational purpose, more clearly. This sweet spot will look different for each participant depending on their unique Divine GPS and who their neighbors are in each of their domains of life. The more aligned these three circles are, the more significant of an impact a believer will have in blessing others. As an artist mixes three primary colors into different hues and colors, each time creating a unique work of art, so it will be for each participant as they blend these three circles together, trusting that Jesus, the master artist, is, in the process, creating his masterpiece in and through each and every vocational encounter.

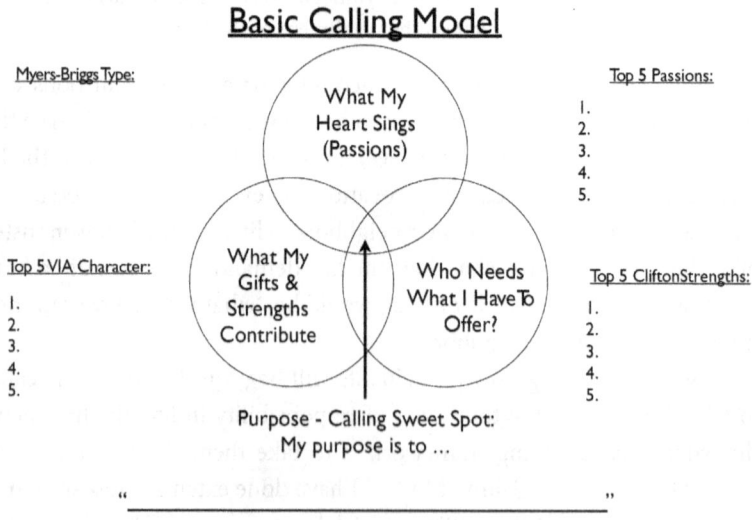

Figure 7. Basic Calling Model

Setting Up the Coaching Project

The goal of having participants go through this Basic Calling Model is to help them better discern their "why" in life. Simon Sinek, in his book *Find Your Why*, discusses the importance of discovering one's "why" in life when he writes, "Every one of us has a WHY, a deep-seated purpose, cause or belief that is the source of our passion and inspiration."[69] As seen throughout this chapter in various Scriptures like Eph 2:10 and Ps 139:13–16, one's "why" is partly found not only in each aspect of their Divine GPS but also in God's gifting and design in their life. Collins addresses this defining of a believer's personal "why" in terms of finding one's life mission when he explains, "God guides in various ways, but most of us don't find our life missions until we are aware of our values, passions, strengths, and vision."[70] For Sinek, articulating one's "why" comes down to filling in the following blanks: "To ____ so that ____."[71] The first blank represents one's *contribution* in service to others, and the second blank represents the *impact* of that contribution.[72] It is only by answering these two things, according to his "Golden Circle" model with one's "why" clearly defined in the center, that the "how" they will go about the "why" and "what" they will do as a result can be answered.[73]

A second coaching tool that will be utilized in the vocational coaching framework is the BLESS© model.[74] The BLESS model is designed to help empower believers to be a greater blessing to their neighbors. I have been granted permission to utilize this BLESS model in my Called2B vocational coaching framework as part of my role as the Executive Director of Wellness and Coaching here in the Southeastern District (LCMS). BLESS is an acronym that stands for bond, learn, engage, serve, and share. According to the model, the first step for believers in being a greater blessing to others is that one must first bond with their neighbor in developing a relationship of trust. Next, there is value in learning their story, both their hopes and dreams as well as their hurts and pains in life. After this, one must intentionally engage in their neighbor's life, making time in the busyness of life to be there, living life with their neighbor. After one engages, believers

---

69. Sinek et al., *Find Your Why*, 4.
70. Collins, *Christian Coaching*, 190.
71. Sinek et al., *Find Your Why*, 35.
72. Sinek et al., *Find Your Why*, 35.
73. Sinek et al., *Find Your Why*, 16.
74. ©2016 Southeastern District. The BLESS Model is part of a larger body of work called iNeighborhood, developed by Bruce Jaeger for the Southeastern District, LCMS.

seek to serve their neighbor at the point of their felt need, reflecting the love of Jesus in practical ways. Finally, only after a bond of trust has been developed does one pray for and seek an opportunity to share the good news about Jesus. This BLESS model can be a valuable coaching tool in helping participants develop an intentional strategy of how they will practically bless their neighbors wherever they live, work, and play in life.

The following are some potential coaching questions to explore this element of empowering believers to make a kingdom impact in their everyday callings in life:

1. If you could paint the perfect picture of your life at the end of this coaching process, what would it look like?
2. If God could paint a perfect picture through your life for the sake of blessing others, what would it look like?
3. What does it look like when those two pictures begin to merge together?
4. (Introduce the Calling Model.) How does your Divine GPS begin to help you fill in the details as to your purpose in life?
5. Who needs what you uniquely have to offer in each of the areas of responsibility in your life? (church, family, lifework, and society)
6. What does your "why" begin to look like when you pull all three circles together?
7. Fill in the blanks: "My purpose is to _____ so that _____."
8. What does it look like for you to uniquely bless your neighbors in each of the stations of your life? (Introduce the BLESS© Model.)
9. How can you more intentionally bond with your neighbors?
10. What things would be important to learn about their lives?
11. How can you free up more time to be engaged in their lives?
12. How can you serve them in a way that meets specific needs in their lives?
13. What would it look like to share the gospel with them in a way that will sound like truly good news?
14. Who could you partner with to be a greater blessing to your neighbors together than you could by yourself?

Setting Up the Coaching Project

15. Now that you understand your "why," how would you go about living that out in love and service to your neighbors?

16. What will you commit to do as a result of this coaching conversation? What support do you need?

Bringing It All Together—Called2B Coaching Dashboard

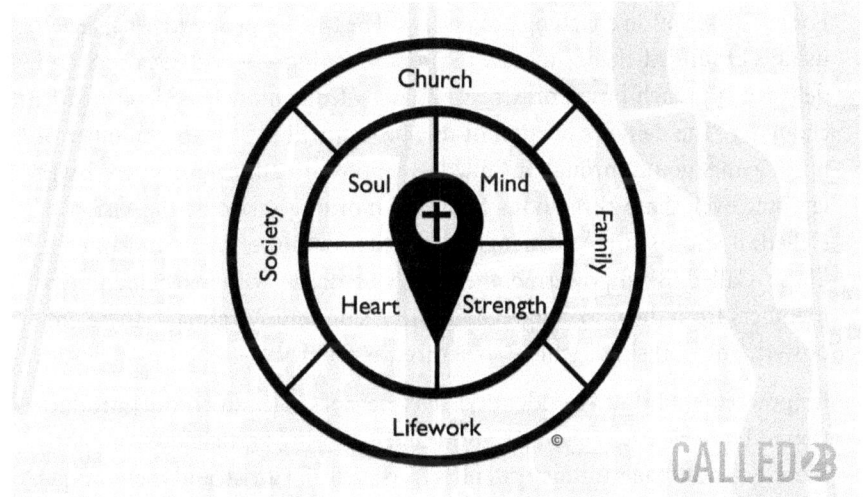

Figure 8. Called2B Coaching Dashboard

To bring all of this Called2B coaching framework together, I have developed what I am calling the "Called2B Coaching Dashboard." This coaching tool is a visual representation of this Called2B vocational coaching process, metaphorically serving as both a compass to navigate living out a believer's calling in Christ in all of their areas of responsibility in life, as well as serving as a gyroscope to help keep them balanced as they do. The cross at the coaching wheel's center represents a participant's ultimate identity in Christ. Just like a GPS device for one's car or phone would be useless without maps loaded in, so a believer's identity in Christ serves as a map for life, reminding them who they are and what life is all about. The GPS symbol reminds participants of their unique identity of God's workmanship, gifting, and design in their life—their Divine GPS—which serves as a compass to help navigate life's callings and responsibilities. The inner "Heart, Soul,

Mind, Strength" circle serves as a visual reminder, like a fuel gauge in a car, that they need to be empowered for life's journey. Finally, the outer circle represents the four stations, or domains, of a believer's calling in their horizontal relationships with their neighbors. This outer circle also serves as a sort of gyroscope, reminding believers of the importance of keeping balance in life.

LAYING OUT THE DISSERTATION COACHING PROJECT

For my dissertation coaching project, I will be taking a qualitative approach using a grounded-theory model.[75] I propose taking a hybrid discovery and delivery approach based on Creswell's knowledge model, as described in chapter 3. The delivery portion of this project will start with a number of participants going through a Called2B empowerment event, where I will lay out, over three three-hour Saturday morning sessions, the vision of Called2B and its three elements of Identity, Empowerment, and Impact. These Called2B empowerment events will occur with participation of members from the C10 congregations in Richmond, Virginia.[76] These empowerment workshops will be structured as follows:

Empowerment Event #1—Identity: Overview of Called2B vision, introduction to Luther's teaching on vocation, and exploring participant's authentic Identity—both their ultimate identity, vertically in Christ, and their unique identity, of God's workmanship and gifting.

Empowerment Event #2—Empowerment: Empowering participants to form strengths-based teams and ministries, and empowering participants' heart, soul, mind, and strength to live out their calling in Christ in all of their callings in life.

Empowerment Event #3—Impact: Exploring with participants how they can live out their authentic calling in Christ to love and serve their neighbors more intentionally in their various areas of responsibility in life (church, family, lifework, and society) for a greater kingdom impact.

---

75. Creswell, *Qualitative Inquiry*, 85.

76. C10 is an association of LCMS congregations in the Richmond, Virginia, area focused on five key outcomes: (1) equip the Priesthood of All Believers, (2) plan joint service activities for the community, (3) coordinate shared services among partner congregations, (4) implement a joint communication strategy to increase awareness of C10 churches in the greater-Richmond area, and (5) begin new outside-the-box mission starts.

Setting Up the Coaching Project

After these three Called2B empowerment events, ten individuals will be invited to participate in the discovery portion of this dissertation project to go through the Called2B vocational coaching framework I have laid out here in chapter 4. This coaching process will help further deepen the awareness of what participants have learned during the Called2B empowerment events to better understand their authentic calling in Christ and personally apply it to their lives in practical ways. This coaching process will also empower participants to live out their authentic calling in Christ, in their various domains of life, and to more intentionally aim their Divine GPS to love and serve their neighbors. As part of this Called2B coaching framework, participants will be invited to take the MBTI, VIA, and the CliftonStrengths assessments, along with the passion assessment I developed for this coaching process. Participants will be asked to commit to twelve sessions of coaching as part of this dissertation project, which will be structured as follows:

Coaching Session #1—Coaching on Participant's Unique Identity in Christ

Coaching Session #2—Coaching on Temperament (MBTI Step II assessment)

Coaching Session #3—Coaching on Character (VIA assessment)

Coaching Session #4—Coaching on Passion (passion assessment)

Coaching Session #5—Coaching on God-Given Talents (CliftonStrengths® assessment)[77]

Coaching Session #6—Coaching on Empowerment (4 Aspects of Self Wheel and empowerment plan)

Coaching Session #7—Coaching on Calling (Basic Calling model and BLESS model)

Coaching Session #8—Coaching on Calling in Church

Coaching Session #9—Coaching on Calling in Family

Coaching Session #10—Coaching on Calling in Lifework

Coaching Session #11—Coaching on Calling in Society

Coaching Session #12—Review and Celebration

After completing this dissertation coaching project, ten participants who just went through the Called2B empowerment event alone will be

---

77. Gallup®, CliftonStrengths® and the CliftonStrengths 34 Themes of Talent are trademarks of Gallup, Inc. All rights reserved.

surveyed on their experience. Additionally, the ten participants in the Called2B vocational coaching framework will also be interviewed on their experience through the whole process, both their experience in the empowerment events and the vocational coaching. My interest is to discover what impact, if any, the addition of a follow-up coaching process provided for discerning and living out one's calling in Christ in order to be a greater blessing to their neighbors, as opposed to those who simply went through the workshops? For each of these groups, I will be inquiring on the following questions to assess the impact of both the delivery (Called2B empowerment events) and discovery (Called2B vocational coaching framework) processes in empowering participants to discover and, more intentionally, live out their calling in Christ to be a greater blessing to their neighbors:

Survey Questions for Called2B Empowerment Event Participants:

Question #1—On a scale of 1 to 10 (1 being low and 10 being high) what was your understanding of your calling in Christ before you started? As a result of the Called2B empowerment events, how would you rank yourself now?

Question #2—How has your understanding of your calling in Christ deepened during this process?

Question #3—How has your understanding of your ultimate identity in Christ, by grace through faith, grown due to this process?

Question #4—How have you grown in your awareness of God's workmanship and gifting as a result of this process?

Question #5—In what ways do you feel more empowered heart, soul, mind, and strength to live out your calling in Christ after this process?

Question #6—How has your understanding of who your neighbor is changed as a result of this process?

Question #7—How are you different as a result of this process?

Survey Questions for Called2B Vocational Coaching Participants:

Question #1—On a scale of 1 to 10 (1 being low and 10 being high) what was your understanding of your calling in Christ before you started?

As a result of the Called2B empowerment events and the Called2B vocational coaching, how would you rank yourself now?

Question #2—How has your understanding of your calling in Christ deepened during this process?

Question #3—How has your understanding of your ultimate identity in Christ, by grace through faith, grown due to this process?

Question #4—How have you grown in your awareness of God's workmanship and gifting as a result of this process?

Question #5—In what ways do you feel more empowered heart, soul, mind, and strength to live out your calling in Christ after this process?

Question #6—How has your understanding of who your neighbor is and what their needs are changed as a result of this process?

Question #7—How are you different now as a result of this process?

Question #8—What were the benefits of going through the follow-up Called2B vocational coaching rather than just going through the Called2B empowerment events alone?

5

Project Results and Interviews

INTRODUCTION—COACHING MATT

When I started this dissertation process, I initially had the idea of taking a case study approach. I wanted to tell the stories of three millennials I had previously coached to explore the impact coaching had on discovering and living out their callings in Christ in all of their areas of responsibility in life. One of these individuals was a young man named Matt.[1] Matt was a twenty-eight-year-old when I first met him, and struggling to figure out what to do with his life. He had many ideas of what he wanted to do, but couldn't settle on one path. Over many months of coaching together, Matt gained clarity about his gifts, passion, and strengths in life, as well as what it would look like to live those out in service to others. Our coaching together provided the clarity he needed to set a path in his life to start moving forward.

In the process of our coaching together, he also started exploring his faith. Like many of his generation, he was a Christian nomad—a believer in Jesus, but disconnected from the church. However, during our coaching sessions, he started exploring how to strengthen his faith in Christ and what it would look like to live it out to be a greater blessing to others. As a result, he started spending daily time in God's word and prayer, he and his wife got connected to a local church, and he found practical ways to love and serve others in his life. And over time, our coaching relationship transformed into a discipling relationship, as well as a close friendship.

---

1. Story shared with permission.

Project Results and Interviews

Unfortunately, I could not move forward in doing a case study on Matt for this dissertation due to a phone call from his wife in early July of 2019. Tragically, Matt died in a car accident, along with a friend, after a 4th of July party. Most importantly, I lost a dear friend and fellow brother in Christ that day. His passing also caused me to re-strategize the approach I was going to take for this dissertation project. After several months of prayer and thought, I decided upon the grounded theory coaching project I laid out in the previous chapter. However, the reason I wanted to share about Matt here was to, first of all, honor his memory and tell his story. Secondly, I share his story because of what Matt wrote to me a few years after we concluded our coaching work together.

In a Christmas card Matt sent me a few years before his passing, he wrote about his reflection on our time coaching together:

> The gift of your time each week has been one of the best gifts and blessings I've ever been given. It means more to me than you'll ever know. Your guidance and the light you've shed on my life have really opened up my eyes to what's truly important in life. I know we've spent a lot of time talking about me and my life, but your generosity and the way you live your life has been an inspiration to me, and help me to see what it really means to live a Christ-serving life.

In another card Matt sent me, reflecting on our coaching together, he wrote, "I can't thank you enough for the positive impact you've had on my life. Please continue to help others like me develop a relationship with Jesus."

I share these reflections from Matt on the impact of the coaching and discipling that I did with him as a way to introduce the results of my dissertation coaching project. When I first started coaching Matt those many years ago, I was in the early stages of developing my Called2B vocational discipleship coaching process that I have laid out here in my dissertation. In fact, much of its development can be traced to individuals like Matt whom I have coached over the years. It is an honor to pass along the blessing of what I've learned about coaching to help individuals like Matt deepen their awareness of their calling in Christ and empower them to live out their faith to be a more intentional blessing to others in their various vocations of life.

STARTING THE DISSERTATION COACHING PROJECT

As I laid out in my previous chapter, I conducted three three-hour Called2B empowerment events with the C10 congregations in Richmond, Virginia.

The focus of these empowerment events was to empower everyday believers to discover and live out their authentic calling in Christ in their everyday lives to be a greater blessing to their neighbors. Each empowerment event was focused on one of the three elements, or concentrates, of Called2B—Identity, Empowerment, and Impact. In total, we had sixty participants in these three Called2B empowerment events, which were conducted in-person and online, due to COVID concerns.

To help participants discover their authentic identity of God's workmanship, gifting, and design in life (their Divine GPS), we utilized the CliftonStrengths®[2] assessment and the passion assessment presented in the last chapter on "Setting Up the Coaching Project." The reason for using these two assessments and not the other ones I wrote about (MBTI and VIA) is simply because of the limited time available in the empowerment events. The rationale for this decision was I wanted to make sure ample focus was given in processing the significance of these assessments personally, and how they help create greater synergy to build strengths-based groups and teams.

At the conclusion of these three Called2B empowerment events, I approached ten participants to be interviewed, as part of my dissertation project, to explore the impact of these workshops on their understanding of their calling in Christ. I also approached another ten participants to take part in twelve one-hour follow-up Called2B coaching sessions and be interviewed on the impact of both the empowerment events and coaching combined. This represented 120 hours of coaching over the summer. The ages of the participants range from those in their twenties to those in their seventies, and comprised of seven women and thirteen men. In order to keep confidentiality, the group that participated in the three empowerment events alone will be designated P1–10 and those who participated in the empowerment events and follow-up coaching sessions will be designated as C1–10. I intend to present the findings from both of these sets of interviews to identify themes raised by the participants from their two experiences and then compare and contrast the results to see what value, if any, the follow-up vocational coaching sessions provided in helping participants better discern and live out their authentic calling in Christ in love and service to others.

---

2. Gallup®, CliftonStrengths® and the CliftonStrengths 34 Themes of Talent are trademarks of Gallup, Inc. All rights reserved.

PROJECT RESULTS AND INTERVIEWS

CALLED2B EMPOWERMENT EVENT PARTICIPANTS' SURVEY RESULTS

The first question I asked the P1–10 group on their participation in the Called2B empowerment events was to rate their understanding of their calling in Christ on a scale of 1–10 (1 being low, 10 being high) before the empowerment events and afterward. It is essential to note the reason and purpose for this question. While my sample size is not large enough to constitute being able to make a statistical argument regarding the impact that either the empowerment events or the follow-up coaching made, my intention behind this question is to demonstrate, from a qualitative standpoint, perceived growth in the participants' understanding of their calling in Christ. This question's purpose is to gauge how much they subjectively believed they understood their calling before and how their understanding changed afterward. While for P1 there was no change in their understanding of their calling in Christ before and after, on average, there was a 1.9 point or 19 percent increase for the rest of the group. The participant who saw the biggest change from before to after was P10.

Table 5. P1–10's Response to First & Second Question

Participants	Question #1	Question #2	Difference
P1	9	9	0
P2	6	8	2
P3	6	8	2
P4	6	7	1
P5	6	7	1
P6	6	8	2
P7	6	8	2
P8	6	9	3
P9	7	9	2
P10	4	8	4
Totals:	6.2 Average	8.1 Average	1.9 = 19 percent increase

The second question I asked the P1–10 group was "How has your understanding of your calling in Christ deepened during this process?" The purpose of this question was to understand, from an overall standpoint, what change had taken place in their awareness of their calling in Christ and how to live that calling out in their various stations in life to serve others. P2 expressed that the empowerment events were impactful to his overall understanding of his calling in Christ. He noted, "I was struck by the theological basis of my calling, which helped me understand the 'why' behind what I do." P6 and P9 also indicated that the biblical and theological background to Luther's teaching on vocation was helpful in their understanding of their calling. P3 indicated that her participation in the Called2B empowerment events gave her more focus to her callings in life, and P8 emphasized that she had a greater understanding of her calling in Christ as a result of her participation.

It is interesting that, in response to the third survey question "How has your understanding of your ultimate identity in Christ, by grace through faith, grown due to this process?" several participants in this group jumped right into talking about their unique identity of God's workmanship and gifting. However, a few participants expressed how helpful the first empowerment event was to help them grow their awareness of their ultimate identity in Jesus. P3 noted that it was a good reminder to be more engaged in her ultimate calling in Christ. P4 expressed a deeper understanding of his calling in Christ. P8 responded, "I have always resonated with the belief that I played no part in my own salvation, that it is all Jesus all the time, but the workshop brought such clarity and simplicity to that concept." While, overall, there did not seem to be any reality-altering awareness created in this part of the first empowerment event for the participants, P10 expressed that his ultimate identity in Christ was reinforced, giving him a rational reinforcement to his faith. This view seemed to be the overall sentiment of this group of participants.

Responding to the fourth question, "How have you grown in your awareness of God's workmanship and gifting as a result of this process?" the participants gave significantly more feedback. P1 especially appreciated the CliftonStrengths®[3] assessment that all participants took as part of the empowerment events to understand their God-given talents better. He stated, "CliftonStrengths® gave me a better understanding of how I operate, and it gave me permission and affirmation to operate from the best of who God made me to be." He also noted how it gave him an appreciation of how others operate in life as well. P2 reflected on how he was more aware of his workmanship and gifting. P3 indicated that she grew in realizing that

---

3. Gallup®, CliftonStrengths® and the CliftonStrengths 34 Themes of Talent are trademarks of Gallup, Inc. All rights reserved.

her gifts were unique and that she needs to partner with others who have complementary gifts to accomplish more effectively.

Continuing on, P6 shared that he had a better understanding of his skills and abilities and how they apply to his callings in life, as well as a better appreciation for the strengths and abilities of others. P7 commented that he now better understands how it takes all of us, with our unique gifts, to get things done, and now, focusing on his God-given talents, gives more direction in living out his callings to serve others. P8 shared how she better grasps that God has specifically gifted her uniquely to do the work he has called her to do and how it can be used for God's glory. And finally, P10 reflected on the impact of better understanding his unique identity of God's gifting and design in his life, through the lens of the CliftonStrengths®[4] assessment, by stating, "The assessment gave me a better understanding of my gifting and helped me focus on my unique strengths. I have been given a broad spectrum of how I can express how I was created."

Reflecting on the fifth question, "In what ways do you feel more empowered heart, soul, mind, and strength to live out your calling in Christ after this process?" P2 said,

> One of the things you focused on was in regards to fruitful living, that rest is important. You have to schedule these things into your life. . . . You have to have that Sabbath rest to get you prepared for the work. I'm really motivated right now—I feel really charged up to do some things.

P3 indicated that she was now focused on living a more balanced life when she said,

> The biggest thing that stuck with me through that session was remembering to balance all four of them, that every single one of them is important. Normally you focus on two or maybe, if you are lucky, three at a time, but to focus on all four you have to be conscious about it.

P3 specifically mentioned that she hadn't been refreshing herself in regards to her mind and spirit for a while and it was a good realization for her that she needed to pay more attention to these aspects of her self-care. P4 indicated that he started setting daily goals according to these four aspects of his self. As a result, this self-care and empowerment was becoming more of a

---

4. Gallup®, CliftonStrengths® and the CliftonStrengths 34 Themes of Talent are trademarks of Gallup, Inc. All rights reserved.

habit in his life. P6 felt that he had personal growth in regards to his heart, soul, mind, and body due to the second empowerment event. He especially appreciated the "4 Aspects of Self Wheel" because of how his mind works; that he can rate an area of his life and then be able to set goals to see improvement was helpful. As a result of the focus of this process, P5, P8, and P10 all indicated that they felt more empowered to live out their callings.

In regards to the sixth question, "How has your understanding of who your neighbor is changed as a result of this process?" there is some indication that there was greater awareness created regarding the idea of neighbor. P1 and P6 both indicated that there was little change in their understanding due to a lot of consideration they had given to this question in the past, while P5 stated that he got the least out of this focus. However, P2 replied that his definition of neighbor was redefined. He now believes that he is much more intentional in being a better neighbor as a result of the Called2B empowerment events. He went on to say, "Not that I was a bad neighbor, but I wasn't an engaged neighbor. . . . I now broaden that view of neighbor as just about everybody."

P3 shared that the impact for her is that now her focus has changed, she is now more intentional in connecting with individuals, rather than just seeing groups of people, because of her relationship-building talents. P4 and P7 also indicated that they had an expanded focus on who their neighbor is in life. P4 specifically shared about his expanded vision of who his neighbor now is by saying, "It's bigger than just the people you live next to . . . your community has gaps and things that you can fill, but don't just limit your neighbor to who lives on your street." P8 responded, "My neighbor is anyone that God puts in my path." Similarly, P9 stated, "My understanding of who my neighbor is expanded greatly . . . I need to reach out to others and share my time, talents and treasures." Lastly, P10 responded, "Everyone is my neighbor and, as a result, the way that I interact with my neighbors has changed."

Concerning the last interview question for this group, "How are you different as a result of this process?" the responses varied. P1 felt that he was better equipped to now help others discover their calling in life. P2 indicated that the Called2B empowerment events gave him an understanding of the "why" of life, with all the shared Bible passages. Further elaborating on the importance of this, he indicated that he often gets so focused on checking off things from his daily "to-do" list that he doesn't introspectively dwell on the "why" behind what he does. P3 indicated that this process had changed her focus on what is truly important in life. P4 responded that he feels like he now has a personal framework to implement in his life.

Additionally, P5 shared that he believes that he is now less afraid to step out of his comfort zone as he lives out his calling in Christ. For P6, he valued a greater clarity of thought on how to utilize his God-given talents and passions for being a more intentional blessing to others. P7 reflected, "It affirmed different things I thought I knew all along. It helped me get some direction and piece together how I can use the gifts God has given me more effectively." P8 felt that she now had a greater awareness of her purpose in life. P9 explained, "I am different in that it has broadened my thoughts of who needs what I have to offer." And finally, P10 reported back, "I have a more complete perspective of my faith and my belief. . . . [I'm] realizing that I have time on earth to do things. I was put on this earth for a reason, and sitting on my butt to watch a TV program, ain't it."

CALLED2B COACHING PARTICIPANTS SURVEY RESULTS

For those who went through both the Called2B empowerment events as well as the twelve follow-up sessions of vocational empowerment coaching, I asked the same series of questions. Similar to the first group of participants, I asked the C1–10 group to rate their understanding of their calling in Christ on a scale of 1–10 (1 being low, 10 being high) before and after both the empowerment events and coaching. The results were rather interesting. Again, while there can be no statistical argument made regarding the impact of the additional coaching this group received quantitatively, there is a significant increase in the subjective view of the impact of this process, in total, regarding their understanding of their calling in Christ. C5 reported a 2 point increase in their before and after response, which was equal to the average reported increase of the entire first group. C2 and C4 both reported a slightly larger, 2.5, increase. For others, the increase is much more significant, with one (C6) reporting a 3 point perceived increase, two (C3 and C7) reporting a 3.5 point increase, and three (C1, C9, and C10) reporting a 4 point increase. On average, there was a 3.2 point, or 32 percent, increase in this group's understanding of their calling in Christ from before and after both the empowerment events and the follow-up coaching they received.

Table 6. C1–10's Response to the First Question

Participants	Question #1	Questions #2	Difference
C1	6	10	4
C2	7	9.5	2.5
C3	6	9/10 (9.5)	3.5
C4	5	7/8 (7.5)	2.5
C5	7	9	2
C6	6	9	3
C7	5	8/9 (8.5)	3.5
C8	6	9	3
C9	5	9	4
C10	5	9	4
Totals:	5.8 Average	9 Average	3.2 = 32 percent increase

There were various responses, regarding the second question, on how their understanding of their calling in Christ deepened due to the empowerment events and the follow-up coaching. C1 indicated that she now sees clearly what she's supposed to be doing in the church. Further elaborating, she stated, "I know exactly what God expects of me and what he has gifted me to do. This is the value of this process—it gave me specificity in what I am called to do." C3 commented that the coaching helped him see that his circle of influence is far greater than he thought, and it helped him understand the impactful role he has in other people's lives. C4 shared that the process helped her fill in specifics and tangibles behind many things that she already knew regarding calling and vocation. C6 noted that going through this process helped him better understand who he is and what he can do. Discussing both the impact of the empowerment events along with the coaching, C7 shared, "This process connected the dots and helped me to see the picture more clearly. The picture hasn't changed, but, like the Claritin commercial, it isn't foggy anymore." He especially resonated with the structure of the workshops and the framework coaching, finding them to be very beneficial. C9 indicated that as a result of the process, he now feels very sure about the direction he is now going in life. And C10 commented that he now has a high awareness of his calling in Christ.

Regarding question three, about how their understanding of their ultimate identity in Christ, by grace through faith, grew due to this process, there were some mixed responses. C8 shared that she felt constant with no change in terms of growth in awareness of her ultimate identity. And, like some of the P1–10 group responses, C1, C5, and C6 jumped to talking about the increase in the understanding of their unique calling of God's workmanship and gifting in their life. However, C2 indicated that her ultimate identity in Christ "definitely grew." Regarding growth in awareness of his ultimate identity, C3 stated that he has a more profound sense that God's grace is prevalent in his life and of how it impacts his relationships with others. C4 shared that the process reinforced her understanding of her ultimate calling in Christ. Likewise, C7 commented on how his ultimate identity in Jesus gained some texture and depth. For C9, he reported that the empowerment events and coaching had a profound impact on him by saying,

> What has deepened for me is being aware of Christ's presence in my life. I didn't always think about this before, but I do now. I had a sense of belonging before, but now I know what that means—I know what it means to be a follower of Christ and a child of God. I feel attached to God and accepted by him.

Likewise, C10 also reported having grown in his faith as a result of this process, stating, "My faith has been brought to a new level. I know Christ's presence in my life. Rather than give faith lip service, I now internalize it."

The question that created the most energy and conversation for the C1–10 group was question number four, on how they have grown in their awareness of God's workmanship and gifting as a result of this process. C1 talked about how knowing her unique identity, her Divine GPS, creates intentionality in what she does. Specifically referring to the follow-up coaching, she stated, "I know that I have a specific unique identity, and it is not a generic identity. The biggest takeaway is looking at each aspect of my workmanship week after week and seeing the nuances of how they work together." C2 discussed how, as a result of the empowerment events and the coaching, she better understands why she does certain things and how it relates to her gifting and design. For C3, what he appreciated about the coaching was how a deeper awareness of his unique identity not only strengthened his relationship with God but also deepened his appreciation of what drives others in ministry teams.

Additionally, the coaching around C4's unique identity had a profound impact on how she now sees herself. She explained, "Coaching helped me to unpack and understand my unique identity. The value of the assessments helped me move away from self-criticism and see how the different parts work together." For her, it boosted her confidence to know her God-given talents. C5 commented about the freedom and confidence she now had as a result of this vocational coaching process by stating,

> My gifts and talents are better articulated, and I now know where I can be of best service. I understand what part of the body of Christ I am and not to try to be someone I am not. I am more comfortable being who I was created to be.

Similarly, C6 discussed how coaching around the various assessment tools utilized helped him discover his God-given gifting and design. As a result, he explained, "It made me ask myself: how can I be a greater blessing with my Divine GPS?"

For C7, he commented on how coaching on the various assessment tools helped him better understand the unique person God made him to be. Further elaborating on the significance of this increased awareness, he stated, "Looking forward, it is easier for me to embrace my gifting and pursue more opportunities to be a benefit to others." C8 also discussed how, as a result of the coaching, she has greater awareness of her Divine GPS and how it helped her apply them to better love and serve those around her. She especially remarked on the impact of the follow-up coaching we did together by saying, "The coaching especially helped to surface the ways that God has blessed and prepared me to live out my calling." Echoing the comments of many in this second group on the impact of the follow-up coaching, C9 indicated how he had greater awareness of the gifts God has given him and how to use them for the sake of serving others. Finally, C10 responded to this question on the growth in awareness of his God-given workmanship and gifting by stating, "Knowing my strengths, I now see them as tools that I can use in difficult times. Coaching helped to bring these tools to the surface. It blows me away that I have more to offer."

Responding to question five, several participants felt more empowered heart, soul, mind, and body to live out their calling in Christ. C2 shared that it made more sense when we focus on these four aspects of self, that it is a more balanced approach to self-care. Additionally, C7 noted that it was beneficial to his overall well-being to think about replenishing his heart, soul, mind, and strength. To this point, he specifically stated, "I feel very well equipped, through this process, to make realistic goals and feel good about achieving them." Likewise, C8 also talked about the benefits of creating an empowerment plan focused on these four aspects of self. She stated, "Setting goals helps me to be the best of who I am. Making the empowerment plan will help me to live out my calling, but the coaching is especially helpful in making an impact." C9 shared that the best part of the empowerment plan is permitting yourself to do important things for your self-care. Lastly, C3, C4, and C5 also expressed feeling more empowered to live out their calling in Christ as a result.

The sixth question had to do with how their understanding of who their neighbor is has changed due to this process. In response to this question, C4 shared that the empowerment events and the coaching increased her perspective of who her neighbor is in life. Also, C5 expressed having a deepened awareness of who her neighbor is by replying, "Everyone I come in contact with is my neighbor." C7 expressed a significant shift in his thinking by stating,

> This process helped me to sift through all the noise and be more effective in plugging into society to be a blessing. Thinking not just about your neighbor but that they are someone that God has called you to love and serve is a big mental leap.

In addition, C6 shared that the coaching process helped her focus more specifically on those around her and how she can be doing more to serve their needs. Finally, in response to this question, C9 stated, "Who is not my neighbor? My neighbor has broadened not just locally but globally."

The final question that I asked the C1–10 group, that I also asked the P1–10 group, was, "How are you different now as a result of this process?" C1 responded to this question by saying, "It has given me a greater sense of urgency in terms of who my neighbor is and being ready to serve them. I feel more compelled to get to work, to do the things that God has called me to do." Likewise, C2 shared that she is now more intentional in reaching out to and serving her neighbors. Expressing a personal transformation he went through in his view of working with others as a result of the coaching, C3 stated, "I am different because it has helped me to be a better listener and appreciate other's ideas and values more." On a personal level, C4 reported that this process boosted her confidence to know her strengths in life. For C5, her response was focused on an internal and external change in her perspective as a result of the follow-up coaching. She explained, "I am more content with myself, and recognize how blessed I am. I want to do more for others as a result." Additionally, C6 reported that due to the vocational coaching process, he is now more willing to overcome obstacles and seek new ways to make himself a greater blessing to others.

Who Have You Been Called to Be?

In C7's case, he shared about the greater awareness he has regarding God's gifting and design in his life, and how this awareness has empowered him to be a greater blessing to others:

> It is so much easier for me to show God's love to others now that I know the gifts He has given me. I have a great deal more clarity on how God made me. I have always kinda known but never been able to articulate it in my life.

For C8, she discussed the difference the coaching made by responding, "The coaching process has helped me to focus more specifically on those around me and what can I be doing to serve their needs." She also expressed giving more thought to her interactions with others and feeling more capable of making decisions about her life. C9 talked about how he was now different due to this process by sharing that because of his increased awareness of his Divine GPS, he can directly relate better with others and vice versa. And finally, C10 shared, "As a result of the empowerment events and coaching, I am more confident in using my gifts. My faith remains strong in spite of my circumstances. God has given me such great gifts, and now I am more fully aware due to this process."

THE ADDED VALUE OF COACHING

In addition to the same seven questions I asked both the P1–10 group and the C1–10 group, there was an additional question I asked the group who received follow-up coaching to try to ascertain the added value that coaching offers. The question was "what were the benefits of going through the follow-up Called2B vocational coaching rather than just going through the Called2B empowerment events alone?" The feedback from the C1–10 group was quite revealing. To this question, C1 replied, "It's just like getting a trainer—with a coach, it brings an avenue to not put off doing, and gets you doing. Coaching lets you put concrete action to those ideas that are swirling in your head." She felt that the coaching moved her to action, bringing focus and the ability to live out her faith to make a kingdom impact practically. Also, C2 found the coaching very empowering and beneficial. In answering this question, she responded, "The positive difference of the additional coaching is that it is individualized as opposed to the empowerment events being more generalized." The individualized focus that coaching provided was important to her. Again she stated, "The weekly coaching kept the focus front and center, and gave a level of accountability. I got more out of it than just the empowerment events alone."

The response C3 had to this question was similar. Regarding the added value of coaching as a follow-up to the empowerment events, he stated, "To me, the empowerment events were great, but if you don't go through the coaching, you are missing out. It is an opportunity for God to open our eyes to be willing to step up and step out." C4, in particular, valued the one-on-one aspect that coaching provides by stating, "Coaching helped me to unpack and understand my unique identity. Having someone to talk one-on-one with (a coach) and knowing that no two people are the same is so valuable." C5 noted that the coaching, in addition to the empowerment events, complemented each other very well. Additionally, C6 highlighted the value of both the empowerment events and the coaching in a way that underscored the added importance of coaching when he responded, "The benefit of follow-up coaching in addition to the empowerment events is like dipping your toe in the pool vs. actually swimming in the pool. The both/and is like hearing a sermon and remembering the lesson. The whole is better than the sum of the parts."

Echoing what the coaching participants had shared in their interviews to this point, C7 talked specifically about how the coaching both deepened the awareness of his unique identity as well as empowered him to more intentionally live out his faith in his various callings in life:

> The coaching experience was at a much deeper level and due to the intentionality of the process, it led me through the journey of discovery. This cannot be achieved in just a group setting. The benefit is, now, I can effectively articulate who I am to others. It has empowered me to feel more willing to take risks knowing that this is how God made me.

Similarly, C8 also expressed her view that the coaching she received after the empowerment events helped her better discern her Divine GPS and how to live that out in a way that the workshops alone could not:

> The benefits of going through the coaching above and beyond the events are specifically learning my individual gifts, passions, and strengths through the assessments, and understanding how those things apply to who I am and how to interact with those that God has placed in my life. Digging down into those things can only come from the one-on-one coaching. The coaching is tailored

specifically to me. I would not have figured out some of the important things if not for the coaching.

Both C7 and C8 valued the individualized aspect that the coaching provided that, unfortunately, cannot be experienced in a group setting.

In reflecting on this question about the value added by coaching over the empowerment events alone, C9 highlighted the power of coaching to create change and movement by stating,

> If I had just done the empowerment events, I probably would have been just where I was in the beginning. The coaching made it real. The event was the investment, but the coaching was the payout. This is what made it meaningful.

And finally, C10 also talked about how coaching created awareness and helped him forward his action in terms of his callings by responding, "The empowerment events usually get put into a box and on a shelf. However, the coaching sessions have brought a heightened awareness and helped me to move forward in his kingdom." C9 and C10 both expressed that while workshops and training like the Called2B empowerment events can be beneficial and informative, they don't create transformation and action like coaching.

What is especially interesting is the juxtaposition of these responses by the C1–10 group about the added value that coaching provides when compared to some of the reactions of the P1–10 group about going through the Called2B empowerment events alone. For example, P2 shared that the empowerment events did not allow him to unpack what he learned. Expressing a similar sentiment P4 stated, "The workshop gave a lot of understanding and education, but I need more practical training." P5 also said, during his interview, how he felt that what was missing was how to live out his calling in life—and then do it. The big question for him was, "How do I initiate what I am supposed to be doing?" P6 felt that a missing component to the empowerment events was formalizing and applying what he learned. Following a similar line of thinking, P7 said, "Information is good, but I need to know how to use it in the real world." For each of these participants in the empowerment events, the missing piece was time to personally and practically process what they learned about Luther's teaching on vocation and how to apply it to their various areas of responsibility in life. Conversely, most of the C1–10 group felt they received this personalized time to process through in the follow-up coaching.

Overall, while the empowerment events were perceived to be excellent and beneficial to all the participants for better understanding the biblical and theological basis of Luther's teaching on vocation, the coaching tackled the question "what does this mean?" and, hence, personalized this understanding and learning for the C1–10 group. The coaching provided one-on-one devoted time for each participant to dig deeper to further unpack their assessment results in a way that the empowerment events did not allow, creating greater awareness of God's workmanship, gifting, and design in their lives. Also, the coaching gave personal opportunities to translate the learning from the empowerment events and the deeper understanding they gained regarding their calling in Christ into action in their various callings in life, in love and service to others. Coaching allowed the participants to connect the dots between their calling in Christ, both their ultimate as well as created identity, and how to live that calling out in their various responsibilities in life in a personalized way. Deepening awareness and furthering action are the two key benefits that the follow-up coaching provided the C1–10 group that the P1–10 group did not benefit from to the same degree.

FURTHER RESEARCH

As indicated in reference to the first question I asked both the P 1–10 and the C1–10 groups, regarding their before and after understanding of their calling in Christ, the results cannot be used to make a statistical argument about the added value of coaching quantitatively. This question was only intended to gauge the perceived growth of each individual and each group subjectively. However, the 13 percent increase in understanding of the C1–10 group (32 percent collectively) over that of the P1–10 group (19 percent collectively) calls for further investigation. A further quantitative study to explore, statistically, if coaching, as a follow-up to workshops and training events, indeed plays an essential role in increasing awareness and furthering action over and above these typical ways of empowering people would be of value. Additionally, it would be interesting to see someone conduct a quantitative analysis to show the impact of workshops or training alone in increasing understanding versus coaching alone or the hybrid discovery and delivery model that I utilized in my dissertation coaching study. Perhaps another study could be done on what would be the impact of just coaching alone versus either a workshop alone or a hybrid discovery and delivery model, as explored in this dissertation coaching project.

Who Have You Been Called to Be?

Overall, the hypothesis and subsequent study of utilizing coaching as a tool to personally disciple individuals in their various callings in life has been of merit, as the results point to not only increased awareness but also a desire for action.

6

Application of Vocational Coaching in the Church

THE JOURNEY OF TRANSFORMATION—JACOB'S STORY

As I started my doctoral studies in coaching at Western Seminary, I served as pastor at St. John Lutheran Church in Idaho Falls, Idaho. During my time there, I took all I was learning about coaching and began developing my Called2B vocational coaching process, and utilizing it with members of my congregation to help them better discern and live out their authentic calling in Christ. One of the participants was a young man named Jacob.[1] When Jacob was going through Called2B, he was in the process of picking up the pieces of his life. He had spent time in jail and had just completed rehab for drugs. Not only was he trying to reconnect to his faith but he was also trying to figure out how to start moving forward with his life again.

Jacob participated in a Called2B empowerment event and joined a coaching huddle, with two other participants, coached by my wife, Stephanie. The empowerment event and the coaching was exactly what he needed during this time. As a result of the coaching, he deepened his connection with Christ and grew to understand his God-given gifts, passions, and strengths in his life. But, practically, this vocational framework coaching empowered Jacob to start moving forward again with his life. Before him, he was trying to discern between two job opportunities. The challenge he was trying to figure out was how to interview for these positions given his

---

1. Story shared with permission.

complicated past. He was coached on highlighting who God had created and gifted him to be during the coaching journey and what strengths he could bring to a new career. As a result, Jacob not only was offered a position with a fast-food company but quickly worked his way up the ranks to become a manager. Jacob described this vocational framework coaching as "transformational" because it helped him journey on a new path in life as the new creation Jesus had redeemed him to be.

There are Dave, Matt, Jacob, and many others, as demonstrated by my dissertation coaching project, each with their unique vocational journeys, within every ministry. Some are passionate followers of Jesus trying to figure out how to live out their calling in Christ in their various areas of responsibility in life to make a greater kingdom impact. Others are disengaged from the church, and even their faith, yet are trying to discover their place in the world and what the meaning of life is all about. Still, others are trying to pick up the pieces of their lives, broken by circumstances and bad decisions, needing a word of hope that their mistakes will not forever define who they are and who they can become. Each story requires a personal discipleship approach to meet them where they are at and help empower them to discover and live out who they have been created and redeemed to be in life. The vocational coaching process I've laid out throughout this dissertation provides an individualized process to translate Luther's teaching on vocation in a personalized and practical way that can lead to a transformational journey.

APPLICATIONS FOR VOCATIONAL COACHING WITH BELIEVERS

In Rom 13:14 (NIV), the apostle Paul tells his readers, "Rather, clothe yourselves with the Lord Jesus Christ, and do not think about how to gratify the desires of the flesh." Romans 13 primarily addresses how believers live out their calling in Christ in relation to governing authorities as they fulfill their areas of responsibility in life, given by God as part of his care and provision in the world, and how believers should love their neighbors in their daily vocations. As believers live out their daily callings in all aspects of life, the apostle Paul calls them to recognize the present time, that the return of Jesus is near. As such, he encourages them to clothe themselves in their calling in Christ daily so that they may walk not in darkness but, instead, put on the armor of light.

Application of Vocational Coaching in the Church

The Called2B vocational coaching framework I've developed functions metaphorically as a hanger for a piece of clothing. Sometimes it is challenging to consider what to wear amongst all the various options, or how it will look on you, until you put a specific piece of clothing on a hanger. Each step in this vocational coaching process provides a way to sort through how one could clothe themselves that day, so to speak, and consider how the believer might properly "clothe" themselves in Christ in their various areas of responsibilities in life. Going through this process allows believers to take a step back and deepen their awareness of their ultimate identity in Christ in a personalized way by answering the question "who am I?" Additionally, it helps believers consider how they can empower themselves to live out that calling in Christ by answering the question "what empowers me?" Finally, it assists believers in prayerfully considering how they can live out their authentic calling in Christ to make a more significant kingdom impact in their various stations in life daily.

As we consider using this Called2B vocational coaching framework with believers, it is helpful to view its application through the paradigm of Luther's teaching on vocation, especially the four stations, or areas, of responsibility in life—church, family, lifework, and society. While no domain stands alone, as each aspect of one's life influences and impacts another, the application of vocational coaching can be utilized within each, with believers regarding a specific focus, all the while recognizing the need to coach on these other aspects of life holistically. And within each particular station, there are several different applications for this approach to utilizing vocational discipleship coaching, which we will consider.

Vocational Coaching and the Church

The first and primary way I envision this Called2B vocational coaching framework being utilized within the church is as a discipleship process with congregational members to empower them to live out their calling as the Priesthood of All Believers in their daily lives. While there is a great deal of emphasis within some circles of the church regarding lay people being the royal priesthood, a practical process to assist God's people to discern and live out this calling beyond Bible classes and sermons is greatly needed. In a sermon many years ago, I recall a pastor, one Sunday morning, confessing honestly to his congregation, "You all have vocations in life; I just don't know how to help equip you to live out those callings." Whether coupled with a specific delivery approach like a Bible study or training, or solely as a discovery approach utilizing coaching to focus on vocational discernment and empowerment, the Called2B coaching framework can be a powerful tool for discipling everyday believers.

More specifically, within churches, this vocational coaching approach can aid congregational members to discern their gifting and fit within the body of Christ. Many churches have their members fill out time and talent surveys, though often do very little with those results. However, utilizing, say, the CliftonStrengths®[2] assessment and the Called2B Passion Assessment as part of a stewardship initiative could help members discern their God-given talents and passions. As a follow-up to taking these assessments, individual or triad vocational coaching could assist members in better understanding how they can serve according to their unique Divine GPS within their congregations. Getting the right people in the right ministries doing the right things that come naturally to them because of God's gifting in their lives will increase membership engagement and congregational effectiveness. Besides just finding the right fit for members to serve, exploration through coaching of new and creative ways to engage in service, utilizing God's gifting and design in their lives, could create new ministries to further the church's mission and vision.

An additional utilization of this vocational coaching framework could be as part of a new membership process to engage those who are new to a congregation into the ministry of a church. Often, churches have classes to review the basics of the faith and the unique theological teachings of their faith traditions. Others review the mission and vision of their congregations. However, in addition to these valuable emphases, having new members participate in a Called2B empowerment event and follow-up vocational coaching, either individually or in a group setting, would serve two important purposes. First, this would provide an opportunity to personally disciple them, regarding who God has created and redeemed them to be in Christ, and then help them translate how to live that calling out in their daily life. Second, similar to the overall congregational stewardship initiative, this vocational coaching framework could be valuable in helping them find how best they can engage in service within a ministry with their God-given talents.

---

2. Gallup®, CliftonStrengths® and the CliftonStrengths 34 Themes of Talent are trademarks of Gallup, Inc. All rights reserved.

Application of Vocational Coaching in the Church

Yet another application of this vocational coaching process could be in conjunction with a congregation's confirmation program with early teens. The Lutheran tradition and many other mainstream Christian denominations have intentional processes focused on teaching young people the basics of the Christian faith (i.e., the Apostle's Creed, the Ten Commandments, the Lord's Prayer, Baptism, the Lord's Supper, etc.). These instruction processes serve as a way to prepare these young people to confirm their baptismal faith. While this review is beneficial to help early teens grow in their faith and understanding of the basic tenants of the Christian faith, as was highlighted in chapter 1, there is also a need to help young people connect their faith in Christ with their everyday lives. Without this connection, the faith of many remains, at best, theoretical, rather than something practical for daily living. Thus, there would be an incredible value in developing a hybrid discovery and delivery model for confirming the faith of young people where they spend time working with a coach. Again, this can happen individually or with a few others to help them deepen their awareness of their authentic calling in Christ and empower them to live out their faith in love and service to others within the church and beyond, in their other callings in life.

Finally, when considering the benefits of vocational discipleship coaching in empowering everyday believers within a congregation, an intentional coaching process could be coupled with leadership development, evangelism, or other training programs in the form of a hybrid discovery and delivery model. In the Southeastern District where I serve, we are currently taking this approach with our SED Lay Deacon Training Program. Through this two-year training process, participants are equipped to be deacons for service within their respective congregations and in outreach to their communities as everyday missionaries. Besides the two years of courses that they are required to take to prepare them for this service, those enrolled in the program also participate in a coaching huddle for two years. In year one, the framework coaching focuses on their Identity in Christ, which includes better discerning their God-given gifts and talents, and on Empowerment, as they are discipled, developing an empowerment plan so that they can be better stewards of their overall well-being—heart, soul, mind, and strength. In year two, the coaching focus shifts to how they can make a greater kingdom Impact by loving and serving those in their community and winning a hearing for the gospel. A similar vocational coaching approach would be valuable in helping those in a specific congregational training apply and live out what they are learning personally.

Beyond applying vocational discipleship coaching with congregational members, there is also great value in coaching pastors and church workers within a ministry. For example, in a recent article sent out by Barna, a 2021 poll of pastors found that 38 percent of them considered quitting ministry in the last year, up 9 points from the previous year; and, only one in three pastors considered themselves "healthy" in terms of their well-being.[3] Also, as indicated by my personal story, many in ministry struggle with their sense of identity, mistakenly thinking that their identity is defined by what they do in their ministry rather than who they are in Christ. Lastly, many in professional church work would benefit from having a coach to help them process through both the opportunities and challenges that daily ministry presents. In each of these situations, vocational coaching focused around the themes of Identity, Empowerment, and Impact would be very valuable to encourage and support those who work full-time in the church.

Besides focusing on coaching with individual church staff, my vocational coaching framework can be utilized, in part or as a whole, to focus on team-building with a ministry team. For example, the element of Identity from the Called2B vocational coaching process could be the complete focus for a whole day of team-building. The group would explore the team's unique identity individually and collectively by examining their Divine GPS using one or more of the assessment tools I wrote about in chapter 4. Or, instead, a ministry staff could spend time away on a weekend retreat focusing on all three elements of the Called2B vocational discipleship process. In either case, individual or group vocational coaching could follow to help them implement what they learned about themselves through the team-building sessions and apply it to their ministry roles.

Vocational Coaching and Families

Beyond the application of vocational coaching within the church, this Called2B coaching framework also has significant application in coaching families. The first application to consider is pre-marriage coaching. Many times couples go through pre-marriage counseling with a pastor before they get married. However, the term "counseling" assumes that there are problems in the beginning of a relationship that need to be fixed. While

---

3. Barna, "38 percent of U.S. Pastors."

Application of Vocational Coaching in the Church

this may be true for some couples, many would benefit from a coaching approach that starts with the assumption that there is good and strength to build upon in their relationship together. Even in addressing potential problems in a couple's relationship, the focus of the coaching would be on how to build upon the couple's strengths in addressing those challenges to help them prepare for their future callings as husband and wife.

The same vocational coaching approach could help married couples strengthen their relationship as husband and wife. Through coaching, they would begin by exploring each person's ultimate Identity of who they are in Christ, individually and as a couple, as the foundation of their marriage. Next, couples would deepen their awareness of each of their unique identities of God's workmanship, gifting, and design, exploring how to leverage their individual Divine GPSs to build a strengths-based marriage. The next step in the coaching process would be to help couples explore how to empower themselves individually and again as a couple, regarding their heart, soul, mind, and strength, to improve personal and marital well-being. Finally, through this vocational framework coaching, they would explore how, together, they could make a more significant impact in their various areas of responsibility in life, in the church, as a family, in their lifework, and in society. While this approach to vocational coaching is effective with individuals, this would be especially helpful for couples to go through together, because what one person does in a marriage can significantly impact the other spouse and vice versa.

Beyond helping husbands and wives live out their calling of love and service to each other, the Called2B vocational coaching framework can be a helpful discipleship process to empower them to fulfill their calling as parents, in love and service to their children. For example, a coach could work closely with couples to focus on who God has uniquely gifted them to be as parents, both individually and together as a couple. Being aware of how God has uniquely designed them, regarding the natural ways they think, feel, and behave, will help them be both more aware and effective in the unique way each will approach parenting. Then a coach could help parents aim their Divine GPS to serve their child(ren) in order to help them grow in their baptismal calling in Christ and start discerning their own calling in life. So often, parents are tempted to pour their hopes and dreams into their child(ren) rather than help nurture and pull out what God has already poured in.

Vocational coaching can also be of tremendous value to teens as they consider their future callings in life. As previously discussed, many teens struggle to connect their faith in Christ to their everyday lives. This struggle is especially apparent when some teens consider what college to go to and what degree program to study to prepare themselves for their future careers. For some, going to a trade school, or through some other vocational training, might be the right choice for them rather than college. Vocational coaching would greatly help emerging adults better understand that their ultimate identity is defined not by what they do but by who they are because of Jesus. Additionally, they would benefit tremendously by deepening their awareness of their unique identity of the gifts, passions, and strengths they have as part of God's workmanship and design in their lives and receiving coaching on what this all means practically, in terms of their potential future career paths.

Vocational Coaching and Lifework

Another practical application of the Called2B vocational coaching framework is coaching believers on issues revolving around lifework. For example, like teens trying to discern what to study in college as they consider their future career, many starting off their work life would benefit from such coaching. Some, unfortunately, graduate and find that they cannot find a job in the field of their degree study. Or, like for my coaching client Matt, they can't decide on a career to choose because they have so many interests and would benefit from someone walking with them as a coach to explore all their options to select a path forward. For some, it may mean adding additional training and retooling to find their desired position. For others, it may mean getting creative in making the right connections, through networking, to find an open door with a company they wish to work for in life. Finally, however, for some, it may mean learning to accept their current job as their calling for this chapter of their life and seeking to bloom where they are planted until God opens another career opportunity.

Some believers would benefit from vocational coaching focused on their lifework because, like my friend Dave I coached many years ago, they are seeking to make a more significant kingdom impact. This desire to make a greater impact may mean exploring ways to love and serve their neighbors more intentionally through their daily work routines. Deepening their awareness of their Divine GPS would also help them utilize the internal

Application of Vocational Coaching in the Church

resources God has gifted them with to be a greater blessing to others in a unique way within the workplace. A coach might help them do some job sculpting by identifying some work responsibilities that others, who are more gifted, could take to free up more time and do more of what they do best. Finally, vocational coaching might help some believers who desire to start their own business or non-profit venture to meet the practical needs of making a social and kingdom impact in their community and the world.

A benefit of the Called2B vocational coaching process is for those who are seeking to improve their work/life balance. Sadly for some believers, their lives are out of balance because of all the time they devote at work in order to try to get ahead or because of unrealistic workplace expectations placed upon them. They may want to dedicate more time to their family, church, and the volunteer opportunities in their community, but need a coach to help them figure out how. Related to finding more balance in their work life is the desire many have in finding ways to improve their overall well-being. Unfortunately, there are aspects of one's personal well-being that can suffer because of their job demands. A coach can assist believers in creating an empowerment plan that helps them focus on nurturing not only their spiritual well-being but also their physical, emotional, mental, and relational well-being as well.

As discussed in chapter 3 on "Vocational Coaching," times of change and transition can be an excellent opportunity for coaching. For Jacob, working with a coach helped him not only reconnect with his faith in Jesus and deepen his awareness of God's workmanship and gifting in his life, but also helped him at a critical moment of transition as he was trying to get his life back on track. A coach can help one navigate both the opportunities and the challenges of life to find a way forward. Vocational coaching can be valuable in various ways, especially for those seeking a new job because of a layoff or exploring a new career opportunity. For example, a coach can help a coachee explore how their gifts, passions, strengths, as well as their previous experience and education can translate into new work environments. It allows the PBC to discern which jobs are the right fit and which are not. This kind of exploration is also beneficial in the development of a job resume. Many employers ask about the strengths and weaknesses of a potential hire. Knowing what one is good at and not good at in life is essential for finding the right job fit where they can feel engaged in their work and be used by God to be the greatest blessing possible in their place of employment.

The final application of this vocational coaching framework in regards to lifework is with those who are or may be getting ready to retire. Again, as discussed in chapter 3, many retirees struggle with a sense of identity, who they are in life, now that they are not working. This struggle is especially challenging for men. Therefore, working with a coach just before retirement can really help believers get ready for their post-work life, to deepen their awareness of their ultimate identity, not in what they do but who they are in Christ. In addition, this vocational coaching process can also help those getting ready for retirement begin to envision how they can still make a difference by loving and serving others in their other areas of responsibility in their lives—with their family, church, and community. Retirement doesn't have to feel like one is being put out to pasture or as if one has no value left in life. There is a valuable kingdom contribution they can still make. In addition, retirees' well-being is an essential factor in how much they can contribute to various endeavors. Coaching around heart, soul, mind, and strength would be valuable so that they can continue to show up at their best in this new season of life, as well as navigate changes that come with age. There are many opportunities for service for retirees and many people who would value utilizing these believers' talents, gifts, skills, and experience.

Vocational Coaching and Society

In the last of Luther's stations, that of Society, vocational coaching can be a powerful way to empower everyday believers to engage in love and service to their neighborhoods, communities, their nation, and the world. By working with a coach utilizing the Called2B vocational coaching framework, believers can begin to understand better the unique gifts, passions, and strengths that God has gifted them with to be a blessing to others. This coaching can start by creating awareness, for individual Christians, of the opportunities for serving others right where they live—in their apartment building, condo complex, or neighborhood. A coach can help empower believers to do this by having them reflect on the following types of coaching questions: "Who is my neighbor? How can I get to know them? What are their needs? How can I best serve them?"

Besides one's immediate place where they live and work, a coach can help believers specifically examine the opportunities to serve in their sphere of influence as well as explore unmet needs in the community, towards which they could leverage their gifting to meet. This vocational coaching approach would also help groups of believers who share a common passion identify unmet gaps in their community. Then, either they could start a new ministry initiative to meet a need that God has laid on their hearts or work together with an existing nonprofit organization that is already meeting that need. Towards this end, a coach would help the group explore how to create synergy by combining their God-given gifts and talents to make a greater kingdom impact together than they could on their own.

The last application of vocational coaching focusing on the station of Society is helping believers explore how they can be good citizens of their nation. This coaching can explore many issues, like how to help address many problems nationally, such as helping underprivileged youth, addressing the growing drug crisis, criminal justice reform, immigrant resettlement, and the list can go on and on. Also, coaching can help believers explore how they can be part of the solution and not part of the problem regarding the growing political and racial divide that exists nationally. Perhaps the coaching focus could be on whether the coachee should get involved in politics by running for office and how they can best carry out this vocation in line with their faith.

An additional citizenship to consider is our global citizenship. Since, unlike Luther's time, we live in a time in which the world is now so much smaller due to air travel and telecommunications, vocational coaching can be valuable in helping believers better discern how to be good global citizens. Potential topics for exploration are: how do believers act in a socially conscious way on such issues as the environment, world hunger, empowering women in undeveloped countries, social entrepreneurship, and addressing poverty, to name a few. And as they do, they can explore with their coach how to keep a kingdom focus that brings glory to God and sees the gospel of Jesus advance around the world through supporting mission efforts domestically and globally.

APPLICATIONS FOR VOCATIONAL COACHING WITH UNBELIEVERS

Beyond coaching believers to discern better and more intentionally live out their authentic calling in Christ in their daily lives, this vocational coaching framework can also be used to reach out to unbelievers by assisting them to explore issues they are trying to figure out in life. Although, as discussed in chapter 2, unbelievers do not, technically, have "vocations" or "callings," as Luther taught that believers have, there would still be value in helping unbelievers more effectively live out their areas of responsibilities in life. In so doing, God's providence and common grace may more effectively flow through them, allowing outcomes like healthier families, greater workplace engagement and business effectiveness, and greater community and societal well-being. And through these relationships of trust, coaches who are Christians can offer a word of faith, hope, and love regarding who Jesus is and the difference he can make when they experience the crosses that are so often associated with our various areas of responsibility in life.

A natural way a Christian coach could begin using the Called2B vocational coaching framework with unbelievers is through the Outside-In coaching approach, as detailed in chapter 3. In this approach, a coach might begin with unbelievers, as one also, very well, could begin with believers, by coaching around how to improve their impact in some of the various stations of life, like family, lifework, and society. While, likely, unbelievers will not explore how to live in relationship to the church, depending on if they had a churched upbringing, this could potentially be a topic that could come up naturally in the process. Again, as covered in chapter 3, a "Triple Loop" coaching approach would be valuable. Perhaps the coachee only needs performance coaching, where they need to take some new actions to see improvement in the various areas of their life. If performance coaching fails, the coach could move to more strategic coaching to help the PBC think differently about their life situation, leading to potential new actions.

If performance and strategic coaching do not produce the desired results for the client, transformational coaching focused on their identity may be very appropriate. Here, a Christian who is living out their vocation as a coach can help their unbelieving coachee explore some of the deep questions of life, like "who am I?"; "why am I here?"; "what is the meaning of life?" This natural progression of coaching from the outside-in, which I have experienced several times myself coaching non-Christians, is a natural way to explore the deep questions of life and faith that often do not happen if one is serving vocationally as a pastor. Often, when I have engaged unbelievers wearing my "pastor hat," the conversation shuts down because there is a perception that I am trying to do something to them based on my agenda. However, when I have engaged unbelievers wearing my "coaching hat," there is an assumption by the person I am coaching that I am trying to help them with their agenda. Through this trusting coach/coachee relationship, opportunities can develop to share the good news of Jesus and how he makes a difference in this life and for eternity.

The other approach that can be very effective in coaching unbelievers is by taking an Inside-Out approach. In this approach to vocational coaching, the coachee comes to seek a coach because they know that life is not working out for them and they want to make changes. The starting place for this coaching is not with the element of Impact but with Identity by starting with the question "who am I?" A place that I have begun in the past in these situations as a coach is by exploring an individual's unique identity of God's workmanship and design in their lives. One time, I was coaching a young millennial who was struggling in his lifework. He had gone to college but, because of the 2008 economic downturn, there were no jobs in his chosen career path. He was discouraged and looking for some hope in his life. As part of our coaching, I had him take the CliftonStrengths®[4] assessment, and we explored his "gifting" and "design" together. My intentional language in my coaching led him to begin asking the following question during our coaching sessions: "If I have been specifically gifted in this way, then who is the one who gave me these gifts?" This exploration of his God-given talents and strengths in his life also gave him the encouragement and confidence he needed to start looking for a job again.

Finally, this vocational coaching framework could be used in reaching out and ministering to unbelievers by focusing on the Called2B element of Empowerment. Many people today recognize that they need to focus on improving their overall well-being, especially coming out of the Covid-19 pandemic. This work can be approached either by outside-in coaching, concentrating first on simple things they can do to improve their well-being, or by inside-out coaching, focusing on fundamental things that need to change within themselves that will lead to improved well-being. An excellent tool for coaching both unbelievers and believers alike, to improve their overall well-being, is Seligman's PERMA model (positive emotions, engagement, good relationships, meaning, and accomplishments), discussed in chapter 3. A variation of this PERMA model is the PERMA-V model, developed and utilized by St. Andrew's College in Christchurch, New Zealand, as a framework for their positive education philosophy.[5] The "V" in this well-being model represents "vitality," which accounts for

---

4. Gallup®, CliftonStrengths® and the CliftonStrengths 34 Themes of Talent are trademarks of Gallup, Inc. All rights reserved.

5. St. Andrew's, "PERMA-V."

things like sleep, eating right, and exercise. As this PERMA-V model is utilized in conjunction with the Four Aspects of Self (Heart, Soul, Mind, and Strength) from my Called2B vocational coaching model, there is ample opportunity to deepen awareness in unbelievers as to why they aren't doing well in their overall well-being. This coaching approach can open the door to explore the condition of their soul and, potentially, create an opportunity to share the gospel of Jesus.

FINAL THOUGHTS

The purpose of this dissertation was to demonstrate how coaching can help empower believers to discover and live out their authentic calling in Christ in love and service to one's neighbors in their various areas of responsibility in life. For so long, Luther's teaching on vocation has been like a treasure, hidden away out of sight or sitting on a fireplace mantel, that one can observe but cannot touch. Throughout this journey, I've attempted to highlight the value of Luther's teaching that every believer has a holy calling in Christ that is to be lived out in daily life. I've also sought to show how coaching can be a personalized and practical process to help believers be a greater blessing to the neighbors whom God has placed before them in their everyday lives. Through the Called2B vocational coaching framework I've developed, believers can gain a more grounded sense of their identity in Christ and a more profound sense of meaning and purpose that so many lack and desire. Vocational coaching can serve as a vital tool to empower and release the Priesthood of All Believers—a central tenant of the Reformation movement—to be the Church in a way that many, including Luther, always desired to see realized.

A closing thought that I would like to share comes from the writer of the book of Heb 12:1–2 (ESV), in which we hear this word of encouragement:

> Therefore, since we are surrounded by so great a cloud of witnesses, let us also lay aside every weight, and sin which clings so closely, and let us run with endurance the race that is set before us, looking to Jesus, the founder and perfecter of our faith, who for the joy that was set before him endured the cross, despising the shame, and is seated at the right hand of the throne of God.

In this Scripture, we are called to run the race of faith, keeping our eyes focused on Jesus, who has already won the victory for us by his life, death, and resurrection. However, while eternal life awaits all who are saved by

Application of Vocational Coaching in the Church

grace through faith in Jesus as our ultimate victory, we still run through this life of vocation, in which we have various areas of responsibility we are called to carry out in love and service to others.

When I was younger, I used to run cross-country and track. I was an outstanding runner back in the day, winning the state title in cross-country and both the 1,600- and 3,200-meters, in track in the state of Idaho, my senior year. However, I did not achieve success as a runner alone. I had coaches who worked with me to set goals, bring out the best of my talent as a runner, and encouragement when I was discouraged. One of my cross-country and track coaches, John Gibbs, not only helped bring out the best of me athletically but also invested in my life personally and spiritually. During this time, I was coming to faith in Jesus. I had come from a broken home filled with substance abuse and minimal faith background. This family dysfunction impacted me academically. In my eighth-grade year, I got 3 F's, a C, and an A in P. E. because I could run fast. I did not see a lot of value in myself and I felt hopeless. However, John helped me harness my talent for running, helped me find value in myself, and helped me grow in my new faith in Jesus. While I did not continue pursuing a career as a runner, the investment that John made in me as my coach, along with others represented by that great cloud of witnesses that this passage from Hebrews talks about, was invaluable to my life. They helped me grow both in my vertical calling in Christ and also helped prepare me for my future horizontal calling as a pastor and as a coach myself.

Wouldn't it be incredible to have individuals like my former cross-country and track coach walking alongside believers as vocational coaches, helping coach them personally in this race of faith and life we are all called to in Jesus? How invaluable it would be to have coaches help Christians of all ages deepen their awareness of their ultimate as well as their unique identity in Christ. What kind of difference would it make to have those who are trained as faith and life coaches assist believers in developing an empowerment plan so that they can better care for their well-being in terms of their heart, soul, mind, and strength? Imagine the kind of impact—not only within the church but also within families, in the workplace, in our communities, and in the world—if we had individuals equipped as coaches helping believers connect the dots of how to live out their faith in Jesus in their everyday callings in life. Fortunately, we don't have to imagine anymore. Ad Dei gloriam!

Appendix

REGARDING LUTHER'S EXPLANATION ON *vocatio* that goes beyond the New Testament's use of *klesis*, there are no specific "callings" found within Scriptures other than God's calling of Abraham to be the father of many nations and the calling of specific prophets in the Old Testament, such as Isaiah, Jeremiah, Samuel, and Ezekiel, through visions, to perform specific "churchly" tasks. Hence, when Luther defined the term *vocatio*, he not only included the hierarchical structure of the clerical status as a special designation for work within the church, but also applied its use to the various responsibilities in the other two medieval estates among the *ecclesia*, the *politia* or "society," especially its political or ruling arm, and in the *oeconomia*, which is the "household," where Luther made the distinction between family and economic responsibilities. For the biblical foundation of these spheres of life and responsibilities, Luther looked to Scripture, as explained in his "Table of Christian Callings" in the *Small Catechism*. Luther does not provide an exegetical exposition, per say, on his teaching on vocation. He merely draws primarily on God's purpose and will as revealed within the Scripture for human living and flourishing. Ultimately, the concept of "calling," not unlike the concept of "the Trinity," is really an ecclesiastical shorthand for understanding how God works both within the vertical sphere of one's relationship with him through faith in Christ and the horizontal sphere of life in and through each person's areas of responsibility.

Bibliography

Anderson, Diana, and Merrill Anderson. *Coaching That Counts: Harnessing the Power of Leadership Coaching to Deliver Strategic Value*. London: Routledge, 2011.
Auerbach, Jeffery. "An Introduction to Wellness Coaching." Whitepaper, College of Executive Coaching, 2014. https://www.executivecoachcollege.com/downloads/Whitepaper_WellnessCoachingByJeffAuerbach.pdf.
———. *Personal and Executive Coaching: The Complete Guide for Mental Health Professionals*. Ventura, CA: Executive College Press, 2001.
Bacon, Terry, and Laurie Voss. *Adaptive Coaching*. Boston: Nicholas Brealey International, 2012.
Barna. "38% of U.S. Pastors Have Thought about Quitting Full-Time Ministry in the Past Year." Accessed Nov. 16, 2021. https://www.barna.com/research/pastors-well-being.
Barna Group. *Better Together*. Ventura, CA: Barna, 2020.
———. *Christians at Work: Examining the Intersection of Calling and Career*. Ventura, CA: Barna, 2018.
Barna Group and Impact 360 Institute. *Gen Z: The Culture, Beliefs, and Motivations Shaping the Next Generation*. Ventura, CA: Barna, 2018.
Bellah, Robert, et al. *Habits of the Heart: Individualism and Commitment in American Life*. Berkeley, CA: University of California Press, 2008.
Benne, Robert. *Ordinary Saints: An Introduction to the Christian Life*. Minneapolis: Augsburg Fortress, 2003.
Bergquist, William, and Agnes Mura. *Coachbook: A Guide to Organizational Coaching Strategies and Practices*. Self-published, 2011.
Biermann, Joel. *A Case for Character*. Minneapolis: Fortress, 2014.
Biswas-Diener, Robert, and Ben Dean. *Positive Psychology Coaching: Putting the Science of Happiness to Work for Your Clients*. Hoboken, NJ: Jon Wiley, 2007.
Buckingham, Marcus, and Donald O. Clifton. *Now, Discover Your Strengths*. New York: Free Press, 2001.
Buechner, Frederick. *Wishful Thinking: A Theological ABC*. San Francisco: Harper & Row, 1973.
Calvin, John. "Institutes of the Christian Religion." In *Callings: Twenty Centuries of Christian Wisdom on Vocation*, edited by William Placher, 232–38. Grand Rapids: Eerdmans, 2005.

Bibliography

Clifton, Jim, and Sangeeta Badal. *Born to Build: How to Build a Thriving Startup, a Winning Team, New Customers and Your Best Life Imaginable*. New York: Gallup, 2018.

Collins, Gary R. *Christian Coaching: Helping Others Turn Potential into Reality*. Colorado Springs, CO: NavPress, 2002.

Creswell, Jane. *Christ-Centered Coaching: 7 Benefits for Ministry Leaders*. St. Louis: Chalice, 2006.

———. *Coaching for Excellence*. New York: Alpha, 2008.

Deutschman, Alan. *Change or Die*. New York: HarperCollins, 2007.

Dodwell, Tessa. "Coaching Needs to Differ before and after the Transition to Retirement." Special Issue, *International Journal of Evidence Based Coaching and Mentoring* 14 (2020) 102–18. https://radar.brookes.ac.uk/radar/items/ed14033d-43ea-4ccf-b73f-a0ec1374c052/1.

Duncan, Paul. "Examining How the Beliefs of Christian Coaches Impact Their Coaching Practice." Special Issue, *International Journal of Evidence Based Coaching and Mentoring* 6 (June 2012) 30–45. https://radar.brookes.ac.uk/radar/items/93466356-d94b-43c6-a10f-4b32f7cd6b64/1.

Eblin, Scott. *Overworked and Overwhelmed*. Hoboken, NJ: Wiley, 2014.

Froehlich, Karlfried. "Luther on Vocation." *Luther Quarterly* 13 (1999) 195–207.

Gallup. "Learn How the CliftonStrengths Assessment Works." Accessed June 16, 2019. https://www.gallup.com/cliftonstrengths/en/253676/how-cliftonstrengths-works.aspx.

———. *State of the American Workplace*, 2017. https://www.gallup.com/workplace/238085/state-american-workplace-report-2017.aspx.

Gallwey, W. Timothy. *The Inner Game of Tennis*. New York: Random House, 2008.

Gempf, Conrad. *Jesus Asked*. Grand Rapids: Zondervan, 2003.

Green, Suzy. "Positive Psychology Coaching." Paper presented at the Evidence in Action Conference, International Positive Psychology Assosciation (IPPA), March 19, 2021. Online.

Hall, Chad, et al. *Faith Coaching*. Hickory, NC: Coach Approach Ministries, 2009.

Hamen-Kieffer, Gabrielle. *Thriveorship*. Edina, MN: Beaver's Pond, 2005.

Hanssmann, Elke. "Providing Safe Passage into a Larger Life: Supporting Clients' Transformational Change through Coaching." Special Issue, *International Journal of Evidence Based Coaching and Mentoring* 8 (2014) 24–38. https://radar.brookes.ac.uk/radar/items/8843bb0a-1143-4422-b000-060af84344f3/1.

Hargrove, Robert. *Masterful Coaching*. San Francisco: Jossey-Bass, 2008.

Hudson, Frederic. "Context of Coaching." *The International Journal of Coaching in Organizations* 1 (2008) 5–23.

———. *The Handbook of Coaching: A Comprehensive Resource Guide for Managers, Executives, Consultants, and Human Resource Professionals*. San Francisco: Jossey-Bass, 1999.

International Coach Federation (ICF). "About ICF." Accessed July 8, 2020. https://coachfederation.org/about.

———. "ICF Core Competencies." Accessed Aug. 13, 2020. https://coachfederation.org/core-competencies.

———. "Previous Minimum Skills Requirements." Accessed Aug. 10, 2020. https://coachfederation.org/msr.

———. "What Is Professional Coaching?" ICF Coaching FAQs. Accessed July 30, 2016. https://coachfederation.org/about/faqs.

Bibliography

Kiersey, David. *Please Understand Me II*. Del Mar, CA: Prometheus Nemesis, 1998.

Kim, David H. *20 and Something: Have the Time of Your Life (and Figure It All Out Too)*. Grand Rapids: Zondervan, 2013.

Kimsey-House, Henry, et al. *Co-Active Coaching*. Boston: Nicholas Brealey, 2011.

Kinnaman, David. *You Lost Me: Why Young Christians Are Leaving Church and Rethinking Faith*. Grand Rapids: Baker, 2011.

Kinnaman, David, and Mark Matlock. *Faith for Exiles: 5 Ways for a New Generation to Follow Jesus in Digital Babylon*. Grand Rapids: Baker, 2019.

Kolden, Marc. *The Christian's Calling in the World*. St. Paul, MN: Centered Life, 2002.

———. "Luther on Vocation." *Word and World* 3.4 (1983) 382–90.

Kuehne, Dale S. *Sex in the iWorld: Rethinking Relationships beyond an Age of Individualism*. Grand Rapids: Baker Academic, 2009.

Lakies, Chad. "Identity." In *Who Am I? Exploring Your Identity through Your Vocations*, edited by Scott Ashmon, 6–7. Irvine, CA: Fifteen-Seventeen, 2020.

Logan, Robert E., and Sherilyn Carlton. *Coaching 101: Discover the Power of Coaching*. St. Charles, IL: ChurchSmart Resources, 2003.

Louw, J. P., and E. A. Nida. *Greek-English Lexicon of the New Testament: Based on Semantic Domains*. 2nd ed. Vol. 1. New York: United Bible Societies, 1996. Electronic ed.

Luther, Martin. "An Open Letter to the Christian Nobility of the German Nation Concerning the Reform of the Christian Estate." In *Callings: Twenty Centuries of Christian Wisdom on Vocation*, edited by William Placher, 211–12. Grand Rapids: Eerdmans, 2005.

———. "Bondage of the Will, 1525." In *Martin Luther's Basic Theological Writings*, edited by Timothy F. Lull, 218. Minneapolis: Augsburg Fortress, 1989.

———. "Bondage of the Will." In *Luther's Works, Vol. 33: Career of the Reformer III*, edited by J. J. Pelikan et al., 119. St. Louis: Concordia, 1999.

———. "Career of the Reformer III." In *Luther's Works, Vol. 33*, edited by J. J. Pelikan et al. Philadelphia: Fortress, 1999.

———. "The Christian in Society II." In *Luther's Works, Vol. 45*, edited by J. J. Pelikan et al. Philadelphia: Fortress, 1999.

———. "The Christian in Society III." In *Luther's Works, Vol. 46*, edited by J. J. Pelikan et al. Philadelphia: Fortress, 1999.

———. "The Freedom of a Christian." In *Martin Luther's Basic Theological Writings*, edited by Timothy F. Lull. Minneapolis: Augsburg Fortress, 1989.

———. "The Gospel for the Early Christmas Service." In *Callings: Twenty Centuries of Christian Wisdom on Vocation*, edited by William Placher, 213–14. Grand Rapids: Eerdmans, 2005.

———. "The Large Catechism." In *The Book of Concord: The Confessions of the Evangelical Lutheran Church*, edited by Robert Kolb and Timothy J. Wengert, 377–480. Minneapolis: Fortress, 2000.

———. "Defense and Explanation of All the Articles." In *Luther's Works, Vol. 32*, edited by George Forell and Helmut T. Lehmann. Philadelphia: Fortress, 1958.

———. "Lectures on Galatians, 1535: Chapters 1–4." In *Luther's Works, Vol. 26*, edited by J. J. Pelikan et al. St. Louis: Concordia, 1999.

———. "Lectures on Genesis: Chapters 45–50." In *Luther's Works, Vol. 8*, edited by J. J. Pelikan et al. St. Louis: Concordia, 1999.

———. "Lectures on Romans." In *Luther's Works, Vol. 25*, edited by J. J. Pelikan et al. St. Louis: Concordia, 1999.

Bibliography

———. *Luther's Small Catechism*. St. Louis: Concordia, 1986.
———. "Selected Psalms II." In *Luther's Works, Vol. 13*, edited by J. J. Pelikan et al. St. Louis: Concordia, 1999.
———. "Selected Psalms III." In *Luther's Works, Vol. 14*, edited by J. J. Pelikan et al. St. Louis: Concordia, 1999.
———. "Sermon on Keeping Children in School." In *Callings: Twenty Centuries of Christian Wisdom on Vocation*, edited by William Placher, 220–27. Grand Rapids: Eerdmans, 2005.
———. "The Sermon on the Mount and the Magnificat." In *Luther's Works, Vol. 21*, edited by J. J. Pelikan et al. St. Louis: Concordia, 1999.
———. "Trade and Usury." In *Callings: Twenty Centuries of Christian Wisdom on Vocation*, edited by William Placher, 215–17. Grand Rapids: Eerdmans, 2005.
———. "Two Kinds of Righteousness." In *Martin Luther's Basic Theological Writings*, edited by Timothy F. Lull. Minneapolis: Augsburg Fortress, 1989.
———. "Whether Soldiers, Too, Can Be Saved." In *Callings: Twenty Centuries of Christian Wisdom on Vocation*, edited by William Placher, 217–20. Grand Rapids: Eerdmans, 2005.
———. "Word and Sacrament II." In *Luther's Works, Vol. 36*, edited by J. J. Pelikan et al. Philadelphia: Fortress, 1999.
McLean, Pam. "A Developmental Perspective in Coaching." *The International Journal of Coaching in Organizations* 1 (2008) 24–33.
Merriam Webster Dictionary. "Coach." Accessed July 27, 2020. https://www.merriam-webster.com/dictionary/coach.
Miller, Brian. "Framework Coaching." *CAM* Podcast 118. Accessed Aug. 2, 2020. https://coachapproachministries.org/podcast-framework-coaching/.
Miller, Linda, and Chad Hall. *Coaching for Christian Leaders*. St. Louis: Chalice 2007.
Myers, Isabel Briggs, et al. *MBTI Manual*. Mountain View, CA: CPP, 1998.
Niemiec, Ryan. "Evidence in Action." Evidence in Action Conference, International Positive Psychology Assosciation (IPPA), March 19, 2021. Online.
Paustian, Mark A. "Unleashing Our Calling: Today's Christians Find Fulfillment in Their Vocations." Symposium on Vocation, Wisconsin Lutheran Seminary, Mequon, WI, Sept. 18–19, 2006.
Peterson, Christopher, and Martin E. P. Seligman. *Character Strengths and Virtues*. Washington, DC: American Psychological Association, 2004.
———. *A Primer in Positive Psychology*. New York: Oxford University Press, 2006.
Plass, Ewald M., ed. *What Luther Says: A Practical In-Home Anthology for the Active Christian*. St. Louis: Concordia, 1959.
Quenk, Naomi, et al. *MBTI Step II Manual*. Mountain View, CA: CPP, 2001.
Rath, Tom, and Barry Conchie. *Strengths Based Leadership*. New York: Gallup, 2008.
———. *StrengthsFinder 2.0*. New York: Gallup, 2007.
Seligman, Martin E. P. *Flourish: A Visionary New Understanding of Happiness and Well-Being*. New York: Atria Paperback, 2011.
Siegel, Daniel. *Mindsight*. New York: Bantam, 2011.
Siemon-Netto, Uwe. "Vocation vs. Narcissus." *Global Journal of Classic Theology* 11:3 (2014) 1–17.
Sinek, Simon, et al. *Find Your Why*. New York: Portfolio, 2017.

St. Andrew's College. "PERMA-V: St. Andrew's College Framework for Well-Being." Accessed Nov. 24, 2021. https://www.stac.school.nz/why-stac/well-being-at-stac/perma-v/.

Stein, Steven J., and Howard E. Book. *The EQ Edge: Emotional Intelligence and Your Success*. Mississauga, Ontario: Jossey-Bass, 2011.

Steinbronn, Anthony. "The Masks of God: The Significance of Larvae Dei in Luther's Theology." Master's thesis, Concordia Theological Seminary, 1991. Accessed Aug. 4, 2019. www.reverendluther.org/pdfs2/The-Masks-of-God-Rev.Dr.Steinbronn.pdf.

Stoltzfus, Tony. *Leadership Coaching*. Virginia Beach, VA: Self-published, 2005.

Stone, Charles. *Brain Savvy Leaders*. Nashville: Abingdon, 2015.

Tickle, Phyliss. *The Great Emergence: How Christianity Is Changing and Why*. Grand Rapids: Baker, 2008.

Twenge, Jean M. *Generation Me: Why Today's Young Americans Are More Confident, Assertive, Entitled—and More Miserable than Ever Before*. Rev. ed. New York: Atria Paperback, 2014.

Veith, Gene Edward. *God at Work: Your Christian Vocation in All of Life*. Wheaton, IL: Crossway, 2002.

———. *The Spirituality of the Cross: The Way of the First Evangelicals*. St. Louis: Concordia, 1999.

———. *Working for Our Neighbor: A Lutheran Primer on Vocation, Economics, and Ordinary Life*. Grand Rapids: Christian's Library, 2016.

Webb, Keith E. *The COACH Model: For Christian Leaders*. Self-published, 2012.

Willard, Dallas. *Renovation of the Heart*. Colorado Springs: NavPress, 2002.

Winesman, Albert L., et al. *Living Your Strengths*. New York: Gallup, 2003.

Wingren, Gustaf. *Luther on Vocation*. Translated by Carl C. Rasmussen. Eugene, OR: Wipf & Stock, 2004.

Whitmore, John. *Coaching for Performance*. Boston: Nicholas Brealey, 2009.

Wright, N. T. *After You Believe*. New York: HarperOne, 2010.

www.ingramcontent.com/pod-product-compliance
Lightning Source LLC
Chambersburg PA
CBHW072131160426
43197CB00012B/2068